DOWNTOWN

DOWNTOWN
Our Challenging Urban Problems

❦ ❦ ❦

ROBERT A. LISTON

❦ ❦ ❦

DELACORTE PRESS / NEW YORK

Kelley

TO
Bill
AND
Anne Boucher

Contents

Introduction

WHEN I WAS a young newspaper reporter in Baltimore, I was given an assignment which none of the veteran reporters wanted. I was to cover the Greater Baltimore Committee. This was a new organization of businessmen and no one knew much about it, except that its activities sounded singularly uninteresting. Futhermore, the publisher of the newspaper was an active member of the committee, and reporters have a natural reluctance to attend meetings with their bosses. It makes them self-conscious. They not only have to report what happened but what their employer *thought* happened, a problem which never arose in this case.

The activities of the Greater Baltimore Committee are described elsewhere in this book. This story is told here because it was the beginning of my interest in urban problems. The committee became a prime mover in a dozen Baltimore problems, and reporting its activities led to my own immersion in urban affairs. My interest continued through perhaps thousands of reportorial assignments, a score of magazine articles and several books, culminating in this one.

I hope readers will discover, as I have, that the problems of our cities are fascinating. They are devilishly complex and often seemingly without solution. They are the problems of *today*, and one gets the feeling that one is working on a frontier with all its demand for will, patience and courage. Working on urban problems plunges one into controversy, for the problems of cities are the problems of people—no two of which, seemingly, agree on the nature of the problem or what to do about it. In a word, urban problems are today's challenge.

This book tries to portray this challenge. Another goal has been to present urban *problems* as well as the *solutions* both proffered and tried. Another major goal has been to seek an overview of urban problems, to approach our several dilemmas not as individual difficulties, but as a single problem with common origins and similar solutions. This effort requires some indulgence by the reader. It must be remembered that each of the problems discussed in this book has been the subject of a separate book by other writers. An interested and informed reader should study each problem in greater detail. Yet, I believe there is value in the overview attempted here.

Because urban problems are so controversial, this book may be controversial. Great effort has been made to be objective, but there is some opinion in this book. Many responsible, knowledgeable men will disagree with the descriptions of the problems, the causes and certainly the solutions. More power to them. The younger reader who is perhaps learning about urban problems for the first time need not accept the views in this book as the last word on the subject.

A word about sources. I have drawn heavily on my own original research, only some of which has been previously reported. While I have studied the leading authors and principal secondary sources—and am indebted to them—this book is far from a rewrite of other authors.

I would like to express my gratitude to my wife, Jean, who assisted in many ways; William Boucher III; James Lash; Calvin Kytle, Director of Urban America, Inc.; Gordon L. Hopper, Executive Director, Downtown St. Louis, Inc.; B. R. Stokes, General Manager, Bay Area Rapid Transit District, San Francisco; Philip King and M. Ruth Broom of the National Education Association; Mel Seidenberg of the Urban Redevelopment Authority, Pittsburgh; Karen G. Abramson of the National Association of Housing and Redevelopment Officials; Mabel Walker, Executive Director of the Tax Institute of America; the Department of Housing and Urban

Development; the Federal Bureau of Investigation; the Philadelphia City Planning Commission.

Appreciation also goes to Sterling Noel and Earl Pruce of the Baltimore *News American;* Fawcett Publications, Inc.; and Magazine Management, Inc.; all of which published certain of the information contained in this book in other forms. Finally, most heartfelt thanks go to those scores of individuals from whom I learned so much through the years.

DOWNTOWN

❦ CHAPTER ONE ❦

In Search of Perspective

AMERICA'S CITIES face some serious problems. The most casual glance at newspapers, magazines, library shelves and the cities themselves reveals what they are.

Every city has large areas, sometimes square mile upon square mile, of disheveled and blighted houses, many of them unfit for human use, yet occupied by six to eight persons to a bedroom.

These slums are the raw sores of our cities in which fester disease, crime, illiteracy, unemployment, poverty and mental illness. The despair of the ghetto breeds rioting, burning, bombing and pillage.

The slums are the roots of many of the social, economic and educational problems which confront our cities. But there are other problems. The air is unclean and occasionally lethally polluted with noxious fumes from motor vehicles, incinerators and factory smokestacks. Sewage facilities are inadequate, and thus the rivers and lakes from which insufficient water supplies are drawn are polluted.

Cities are choked with cars and trucks so that simply getting to and from work is an exercise in exasperation and a risk to life and limb. Mass transit by bus and train has declined to a point of nonexistence in some communities.

Many American cities are thus depositories of ugliness and human futility—and the worst is yet to come. Our population is growing at an enormous rate. By the end of the century there will be 330 million Americans, compared to 180 million in 1960—and, it is estimated that one third of them will be jammed into just ten cities, ranging in size from 5 million in Cleveland to 23 million in New York.

1

"This," said President Lyndon B. Johnson, "is truly the time of decision for the American city."

This is a book about these urban problems and what we can do about them. Certain it is that these problems are immense and the solutions often inconceivable. But we cannot grasp the problems or discover the solutions unless we first achieve some perspective. We must find a way to hold these problems at arm's length and examine them objectively. We need to observe the assets of our cities, as well as their deficiencies, and to realize that many of the problems are being and will be solved.

Unfortunately, in their efforts to call attention to urban problems, some authors and commentators have made generous use of an old-fashioned journalistic trick, the "scare story."

There are several variations of this technique. In one, the city editor enlivens a "dull news day" by inventing, for example, a "crime wave." This is done simply by taking all the regular crime news, combining it into one story so that it appears to have greater magnitude, and giving the article more prominence in the paper and a headline in larger, blacker type. Or, the editor "exposes" a condition or situation that has been in existence for quite some time, such as substandard housing, poor hospital services, inadequate school facilities or corruption in a government agency. The exposé has a value, in addition to enlivening the news columns, interesting readers and enhancing the newspaper's image of public service. It calls attention to a problem. But this technique also destroys perspective. The problem cited has no relationship to other problems and little association with civic virtues.

The techniques of scare and hyperbole have been applied almost routinely to writings about urban problems. Thus, the customarily careful *New York Times* could not resist the headline:

BEDLAM FOR CITY MENTAL PATIENTS

Certain, but hardly all, mental institutions have quite undesirable conditions, but bedlam? This is an old, tired, inaccurate cliché.

The *Saturday Evening Post* emblazoned its cover with these words:

The National Scandal of
AIR POLLUTION
IT CAN KILL YOU—and it's costing billions

The fouled atmosphere over our cities is a serious problem, but the chances of its killing "you" even if you live in those cities is remote.

Life devoted a double year-end issue to urban problems under this cover headline:

THE U. S. CITY:
ITS GREATNESS IS AT STAKE

Our cities have problems, but to add the spector of decline and fall helps not in their solution. Even Athens and Rome survived.

Look regularly scares its readers:

OUR HOSPITALS ARE KILLING US
An Alarming Report on Conditions
in many American Cities

CRIME IN THE SUBURBS
A New Wave of Robbery, Violence
Teenage Crime Hits Our Homes

As the city editor used to say, "Scare them a little."

Time devoted a cover article to Robert C. Weaver, First Secretary of the Department of Housing and Urban Development, under this headline:

First Negro in the Cabinet
TRYING TO SAVE THE CITIES

Secretary Weaver is known for his dedication, but it is doubtful whether he conceives of himself as the savior of our cities or that the serious problems with which he is coping constitute *saving* cities. The city will survive.

Newspaper and magazine journalists and their counterparts in radio and television are not the only ones using exaggeration for effect. Author Richard J. Whalen has written:

> New York shows alarming signs of spiritual malnutrition and death-by-inches. It is frowning, tight-lipped, short-tempered, the most nervous city in America. It is a city without grace. It is humorless, able to mock and taunt, but too tense to gain the release of laughter. It is a city that cries "jump" to a would-be suicide perched on a window ledge. The city itself sways on the edge of madness.

Lewis Mumford, a highly respected and often quoted writer on urban problems, described city dwellers as "people who do without pure air, who do without sound sleep, who do without a cheerful garden or playing space, who do without the very sight of the sky and the sunlight, who do without free motion, spontaneous play." Mr. Mumford said the "chronic starvation [for these things] produces lack of appetite. Eventually you may live and die without even recognizing the loss."

Even those who are most responsible about seeking solutions to our urban problems have made use of the scare technique. Urban America, Inc., which is an amalgamation of the American Planning and Civic Association and the Action Council for Better Cities, has published brochures which destroy perspective by concocting monster statistics. According to Urban America, the U. S. will have to erect in the next two generations more new housing than has been built since the country began. By 1980 we will have to find room for twice as many cars as in 1966 and nearly double the nation's water supplies. By that same year the nation will have to deal with 250 million tons of pollutants in the air, an increase of 100 million tons from 1966. To portray the decline of urban mass transit in the United States, Urban America reported there were only 6.9 billion passengers in 1964, compared to 19 billion in 1945. The problem of mass transit in this country is bad enough without such tricky statistics, for 1945 was a wholly artificial year. The country was at war, there was full employment, gas was rationed and no cars had been manufactured for four years. For most, the only way to get to work was by walking or public transportation.

This brief critique of some of the literature on urban problems is not intended to minimize our cities' predicament. On the contrary, the young people reading this book will be asked to find solutions to some colossal problems their elders have ignored for generations. We do face some kind of crisis in our cities, but scare headlines and exaggeration do not help in the search for solutions.

How can we gain a truer picture of our urban problems? The search for perspective can begin with the frequently reported fact that 7 out of 10 Americans live in an urban setting. More precisely stated, in 1966, 67 percent of all Americans lived in or near 224 communities that are officially classified as metropolitan because the central city has a population of 50,000 or more. Put another way, 67 percent of our population lives in 9 percent of our land area. By the year 2000, 80 percent of 330 million Americans are expected to live in urban areas. This anticipated increase in population is the root of most of our urban problems.

But if we look at these statistics another way, the impression is unmistakable that our cities, despite their problems, must offer some attractions to cause people to want to live in them. Our cities of 50,000 and over are not concentration camps to which Americans have been herded forcibly. Americans have a reasonably free choice in their homesites. A person can live in a village, town, small city or metropolis. He can choose farm, suburbia, townhouse or apartment. The fact that so many Americans choose to live in or near a city indicates, to borrow an advertising slogan popular in the New York City area, "we must be doing something right" in our cities.

Why do people live in cities? We could get into a chicken-and-egg discussion of employment as a cause for city dwelling. Do people live in cities because that is where the jobs are? Or are the factories and mercantile establishments there because that is where the workers live? Whichever came first, the fact remains that millions of people move from farms and villages to cities every year to obtain employment. There is an element of choice to this, however. People *want* to live in cities.

Psychologists, sociologists, philosophers and theologians can ruminate on why people gather in cities. Perhaps they want to avoid isolation, feel more secure in numbers, benefit from community life. There are undoubtedly many reasons for the increasingly communal nature of living.

But one reason for urbanization is that our cities, faults and all, are quite marvelous. I grew up in small villages in Ohio, but ever since the choice of where to live became mine, I have lived in or near a large city. My idea of an evening's recreation is a trip downtown to enjoy the theater, dinner in a restaurant, window shopping, other entertainment. I carry on a persistent love affair with the city of New York, the biggest and most maligned of our cities, despite the fact I lived there in considerable poverty and took many of the "hard knocks" it has to offer. Chicago is a delight to me, bursting with energy, conveying what I can only describe as virility and masculinity. San Francisco is a jewel, the love-liest city in our land. Los Angeles? Strange, exciting, militantly unorthodox. Houston is to me raw, untamed, uncouth, a diamond in the rough. Baltimore is staid, conventional, delightfully dowdy, a small town grown big. Washington, Philadelphia, Boston, Atlanta, New Orleans, Cleveland, Detroit, St. Louis, Denver—each of our cities has, despite its problems, a flavor, an atmosphere that makes it unique.

To use the popular parlance, a city, any city is where the action is. The city is bright lights, fun, excitement, entertainment. A city is museums mirroring our past, planetariums linking us with the unknown, concerts, plays, opera, ballet, lectures, if only on a box in the park. In a city we are enlightened, outraged and amused, sometimes all at the same time. A city is hope, symbolized in universities, libraries, hospitals, factories, offices, banks. A city is challenge, the "big pond" where "big frogs" grow. The most talented, ablest and luckiest in all walks of life gather there to succeed, to fail and to be glad they tried. But most of all a city is people, beautiful people and ugly, young and old, kindly and vicious, smart and dumb, sensible and foolhardy, white and black, religious and atheist, people of hope and courage and people who live out their lives in quiet (or noisy) desperation. In the city things happen and people make them happen. The city is life.

Any discussion of the problems of our cities, it seems to me, must begin with the realization that as imperfect as they may be, our cities are wonderful places. We have in our American cities great raw material with which to work. As we talk of slums, traffic jams, polluted air and crime in the streets, we might also consider the cultural revolution in the United States, the popularity of concert halls and art museums, the burgeoning sales of books. We might remember the educational revolution wherein half of the high-school graduates are going to college, many of which are located in cities.

Those who write the scare headlines, prepare the monster statistics and cite the ugliness, poverty and pollution of our cities fail to consider the assets of our cities, their factories, stores, buildings—some of which are beautiful—churches, universities, libraries, hospitals. Cities have highways and terminals and airports and freightyards and seaports—the list could go on and on. But the biggest asset is people, for cities are people, intelligent, sensible, resourceful, energetic. There will not be 250 million tons of pollutants in the air in 1980 for the American people will not allow it. There will not be twice as many vehicles on the streets in 1980 because there cannot possibly be and because Americans will never permit it.

A search for perspective must recognize the strides that have already been made by cities. If no American city has reached the perfection which it seeks, all cities have progressed in solving some of their problems. The success of San Francisco and St. Louis in mass transit, Chicago in education, Pittsburgh and Los Angeles in air pollution, and a half hundred major cities in housing and urban renewal belie the scare techniques and statistical legerdemain. This book will try to maintain some perspective by reporting the accomplishments as well as the challenges.

If we try to place our urban problems in the context of our times, we discover there is disagreement, perhaps even conflict, between the theoretical and the pragmatic. An illustration of this is the suggestion that traffic problems could be alleviated by double-decking certain streets. One level could be used for vehicles and another for pedestrians. The idea has some merit. It would increase the amount of street space. Traffic flow would be accelerated. Pedestrians and vehicles would be separated, a great advantage because the mingling of the two causes much of our traffic problem.

This plan has been sharply criticized by Henry A. Barnes, Commissioner of Traffic in New York City. His accomplishments there, as well as in Denver and Baltimore, have made him one of the world's authorities on traffic problems. He points out that the double-decking of streets would be feasible in a new city, but impossible in an existing city. The area below the elevated street would be essentially a tunnel, denied fresh air and sunlight. Thus, the vehicles would have to move on the lower level and the pedestrians on the upper. Entrances and lobbies of buildings would need to be raised to the second floor. The cost would be enormous and the task would be impossible, for existing buildings are not of equal size. The height of first floors vary from building to building, as does the setback from the street. Many of the structures could not withstand such major remodeling. Mr. Barnes, as a practicing traffic engineer, has had many similar disagreements with urban planners.

The conflict between the theoretical and the practical often centers on the matter of beautification. There is something inherently ugly about a gasoline service station. Architecturally, the gas station is far from a joy to the eye. It produces unavoidable odors and noise. Aesthetically, our cities would be lovelier if no gas stations existed. But urban automobile owners need to buy gasoline and to have their cars lubricated and repaired. Perhaps the gas station can be improved, but it will remain essentially as it is. Then there is the suburban drive-in hamburger stand. Even the most palatial of these appears crass and commercial, and a series of them along a roadway epitomizes the urban sprawl so often denounced by planners and architects. But the fact is that a sizeable segment of the population enjoys the drive-in hamburger stand and finds it useful. The variety of drive-in restaurants, movies, banks, muffler shops, etc., seems destined to remain.

In the chapters to follow, this basic conflict between the theoretical and the practical will be demonstrated repeatedly. There is a theoretical and desirable solution to problems which often conflicts with practical considerations. The proffered solution is too expensive or the residents involved are unwilling to accept it. Frequently, the solution to one problem simply creates other difficulties, as in the case of slum clearance. Tearing down blighted blocks of houses to build new, more attractive housing has often hastened the deterioration of other neighborhoods. The residents of the razed homes moved into other areas, causing overcrowding and blight. Slum clearance may unfortunately set up a vicious cycle that worsens the housing problem rather than alleviates it.

Both the theoretical and the practical have a role in solving urban problems, but they must be amalgamated into the *pos-*

sible. Perhaps our basic difficulty is that we have no realistic vision of the city of the future. We can envision a dream city of attractive spires, elevated and subterranean highways and railways speeding vehicles and people, of well laid-out and compartmentalized industrial, commercial and residential districts, of parks and playgrounds and fresh air and sunlight. But this dream collides with the reality of Manhattan, the Loop, or Sunset Strip. The concrete canyons of Manhattan are present and seem unlikely to change in any significant way in the forseeable future. The steel mills at Gary, Indiana, and Sparrows Point, Maryland, exist and their elimination in the next several generations is unthinkable, ugly though they may be. The vast warrens of surburban houses which ring our cities may be poorly constructed and uniformly dreary; they may turn into the slums of the future while the present slums become areas of high-rise apartments and pleasant living, but the much denounced suburban sprawl is reality. It will exist for generations.

Will our existing American cities look essentially different in the year 2000 than they do today? The realistic person must answer no, but, if our problems are solved, appearances will be deceiving. A long-range view from a satellite might show little change, but a closer examination hopefully will show an increase in parks and playgrounds, the addition of trees and flowers, block upon block of new and rehabilitated housing, cleaner air, and smoother flow of vehicles and pedestrians. There will be some dramatic changes, such as startling new buildings, cultural centers, plazas and monuments which convey the city's pride and enhance its beauty. But the startling changes will be the easy part. Finding places for residents to live and work will be the difficult problem.

Another thought that must go into a discussion of urban problems is that the terminology is incorrect. We are dealing with the problems of people, not of cities. A person wants a means of earning a living for himself and his family. He wants a place to live, food on his table, a means to educate himself and his children. He wants health, fresh air, clean water. He wants to travel from place to place, enjoy the beauty created by nature and man. He wants to worship and to have fun to fill his leisure. He wants safety and protection, independence and peace.

Obtaining these goals is the challenge of life, whether a person lives on a farm, in a village or in a block of tenements. These universal human aspirations take on a new terminology when urban problems are discussed: housing, traffic, mass transit, water, air pollution, health, welfare, crime, beautification and recreation. Actually, these problems exist wherever people live. The traffic problem in Keokuk differs only in degree from Chicago's and is equally insufferable in both places. Housing in Springfield, Ohio, is deteriorating just as rapidly as in St. Louis. Serious problems of poverty, race relations, health, crime, education exist in small towns as well as big cities. Sometimes these problems are worse in smaller than in larger places.

It might be said that the problem of air pollution is worse in cities than in towns, although the belching smokestacks of Fort Ticonderoga, New York, make it far from a desirable place to breathe. The grimy mill and mine towns of Pennsylvania indicate the pollution and beautification problems are not exclusive to our great cities. The water problem certainly exists to a great degree in cities, for the apartment dweller cannot very well dig a well. Too, he is more handicapped during a depression, for he cannot spade up a plot in his lawn to grow vegetables to feed his family.

This discussion of terminology and the extent of the problems is not just playing with words, for, when we visualize the problems as those of people rather than of cities, we can move nearer to solutions. As will be shown in chapters to follow, those cities which have made the most progress in solving problems have worked directly with the *people* involved. Government plays an important role, but only when people—individuals and small groups—have become involved have real solutions been developed.

This is one of the reasons that the gargantuan statistics do a disservice. No one can grasp, let alone do much about, 25 million tons of pollutants in the air, but a belching smoke-stack down the street becomes a meaningful problem and one an individual or a neighborhood can correct. Our national need for 68 million new housing units by the year 2000 is a study in futility for all but the statisticians, but a man can grasp that his block is deteriorating and that garbage is thrown out in the street. Solving his immediate problem isn't very easy, but with help and some leadership he can hope for a solution.

The problems of the people who live in our cities will not be solved solely by federal, state or municipal government. They will be solved by the *people* who live in individual homes, blocks and neighborhoods with some help from gov-ernment. In short, we have to reduce the problems to human terms, not build them up to statistical monstrosities in order to bring the will and resourcefulness of people to bear upon them.

Our search for perspective can help us identify the nature of our urban problems. What is so very discouraging is not only that the techniques of scare and statistical sensation-alism have made urban problems larger than life, but also that there are so many of them. There is a housing problem and a traffic problem and an educational problem and many more. When one runs down the entire list, one feels that Job had it easy compared to our city dwellers. To surrender to apathy is tempting.

With perspective we can see that, in our urban problems, we are combating a three-headed squid that has been ignored so long it has grown to gigantic size. The housing, transporta-tion, pollution and other problems referred to are the ten-tacles of the beast. As long as we keep flailing away at the tentacles, we will have only limited success. We push one away and another grabs us.

As everyone knows, the way to defeat a squid is to aim for the head. Our urban squid has three heads. We have three overriding problems which limit our success against the peripheral problems. In the next two chapters we will identify the three heads of our monstrous urban problems and suggest some weapons to use against them.

CHAPTER TWO

Too Many Governments

IN SIMPLEST TERMS, the three overriding urban problems are power, money and planning.

The governmental structure of nearly all our cities denudes them of the ability to solve their housing, transportation and other problems. The tax bind ensnaring urban areas leaves them so financially impoverished they are unable to carry out, and sometimes even unable to seek solutions to, their various problems. The lack of meaningful planning forces cities into piecemeal, inadequate and wasteful actions which sometimes worsen rather than alleviate problems.

The governmental structure of our cities is the single most debilitating factor in urban affairs. The term "city" is a misnomer. When we say "city," we really mean "metropolitan area," which is a central city and its contiguous suburbs stretching for miles in all possible directions. But even the term "metropolitan area" is a misnomer, for today metropolitan areas overlap. The Bureau of the Census considers New York and Newark, N. J., to be distinct metropolitan areas, when in fact the two are so linked by commercial, cultural and social forces that the separation is purely statistical. In fact, the Eastern seaboard from Boston to Washington—some say from Portland, Maine, to Richmond, Virginia—is rapidly becoming one vast area, usually called the "megalopolis." Other megalopolises are forming in the Great Lakes area and on the West Coast.

When we look at our cities as metropolitan areas, some startling changes occur. The following table shows the 15 largest metropolitan areas, as estimated by the Bureau of

Census in 1965, in comparison with the 1960 population of the central city:

Metropolitan Area and Rank, 1965	Percent Change In Metropolitan Population Since 1960	Central City Population and Rank, 1960
1. New York 11,348,000	+ 6.1	7,781,000 (1)
2. Los Angeles 6,776,000	+12.2	2,479,000 (3)
3. Chicago 6,639,000	+ 6.7	3,550,000 (2)
4. Philadelphia 4,667,000	+ 7.5	2,002,000 (4)
5. Detroit 3,972,000	+ 5.6	1,670,000 (5)
6. Boston 3,199,000	+ 2.9	697,000 (13)
7. San Francisco 2,935,000	+10.8	740,000 (12)
8. Washington 2,413,000	+21.3	763,000 (9)
9. Pittsburgh 2,367,000	− 1.6	604,000 (16)
10. St. Louis 2,239,000	+ 6.4	750,000 (10)
11. Cleveland 1,971,000	+ 3.2	876,000 (8)
12. Baltimore 1,857,000	+ 7.5	939,000 (6)
13. Newark, N. J. 1,827,000	+ 8.1	405,000 (30)
14. Houston 1,695,000	+19.5	938,000 (7)
15. Minneapolis–St. Paul 1,602,000	+ 8.1	482,000 (25)

If we look at our cities as metropolitan areas, we find that, instead of five cities listed as having a population of one million and over in the 1960 census (New York, Chicago, Los Angeles, Philadelphia and Detroit), we have a much longer list. In addition to those already listed, the 1965 census estimates show the following urban places with over one million population:

Atlanta	1,205,000
Buffalo	1,322,000
Cincinnati	1,329,000
Denver	1,091,000
Kansas City	1,179,000
Miami	1,064,000
Milwaukee	1,269,000
New Orleans	1,026,000
San Diego	1,145,000
Seattle	1,187,000

To this list must be added three metropolitan areas which few people think of as large cities:

Paterson–Clifton–Passaic, N. J.	1,288,000
San Bernadino–Riverside, Calif.	1,033,000
Anaheim–Santa Ana–Garden Grove, Calif.	1,111,000

Calling these three "metropolitan areas" may well be statistical gamesmanship. Paterson-Clifton-Passaic lie northwest of Newark, N. J., and certainly belong in the Greater New York area. The two California metropolises realistically are part of Greater Los Angeles. The same statistical magic occurs in several places. The separation between the 634,000 people who live in metropolitan Akron, Ohio, from the 1,971,-000 who live in metropolitan Cleveland is almost entirely on paper. It is like separating Dallas and Fort Worth.

A metropolitan area is more than statistics. The residents of metropolitan areas are inexorably bound. They work in the same factories and offices. They shop at the same stores, travel common expressways and streets, cheer together at the ball game, laugh at the same movies in the same theaters, eat in the same restaurants. They often drink the same water. The smog that befouls the air in the city afflicts the suburbs. The race riots that are so costly in the slums of the city drain the economy of the suburbs. The Criminals spawned in the tenements rob and murder in the outskirts. If hospitals are inadequate, rich and poor, city dweller and suburbanite must make do with them.

Residents of a metropolitan area are joined by all the aspirations and problems of the community of man. Yet in this country they are separated governmentally. The 16 million people who live in the greater New York area are separated into—at last count—1,476 governmental jurisdictions. There are three states (New York, New Jersey and Connecticut), 555 incorporated towns and cities, an almost inconceivable hodgepodge of counties and townships, school districts, sewer and water districts, bridge, tunnel, highway, parking and port authorities—to name a few.

Metropolitan Boston includes the 697,000 people who live in the City of Boston and about four times that many people residing in the incorporated suburban towns of Winthrop, Chelsea, Everett, Malden, Revere, Melrose, Saugus, Lynn, Nahant, Swampscott, Marblehead, Watertown, Cambridge, Somerville, Belmont, Arlington, Medford, Winchester, Stoneham, Wakefield, Reading, Woburn, Brookline, Newton, Weston, Waltham, Lexington, Needham, Dedham, Dover, Wellesley, Natick, Framingham, Milton, Westwood, Norwood, Walpole, Canton, Stoughton, Quincy, Braintree, Weymouth, Hingham, Cohasset and Hull—and that is not a complete list. There are 78 incorporated towns in Metropolitan Boston.

If the simple reading of those place names has been somewhat challenging, it is nothing to the challenge of governing metropolitan Boston. Each of these towns has mayors and councilmen, tax collectors, fire chiefs, police officers, dog catchers. Each regulates its own traffic, maintains its own streets, perfects its schools, inspects its housing, zones its land. The overall needs of greater Boston are lost in the shuffle of local politics. What is best for Quincy may have little to do with the needs of Saugus and what is done in Dover may undo the considerable efforts made in Brookline, but who is to deny the right of either place to govern itself?

Boston is not unique, but typical. With one or two notable exceptions, all our metropolitan areas consist of an array of self-governing towns and districts. There are in the United States—again at last count—3,047 counties, 675 cities with 25,000 population and over, 17,368 cities under 25,000 population, 17,198 townships and towns, 34,678 independent school districts, 14,405 special districts, for a grand total of 87,371 governmental units. That is a truly monster statistic.

The results of this Balkanization of our urban areas are futility and tragedy. A highway contractor in the New York area has reported going through 187 procedural steps before being able to award contracts for a new highway. Los Angeles area residents were shocked some time ago when a sub-

urban house burned down although a firehouse was only two
blocks away. But the firehouse was in another town and did
not have jurisdiction.

"The city is weaker as an entity than it has ever been in
history," Catherine Bauer Wurster of the University of California has written. "It controls neither its shape, its function,
nor its density. It is smothered and paralyzed by it own offspring: the suburbs and satellite towns. The latter are themselves equally weak and helpless."

Another comment comes from Professor William A. Robson
of the London School of Economics and Political Science:

> It is obvious that a large municipality, surrounded by a
> multiplicity of small local authorities of various kinds, cannot
> hope to meet the social, political or administrative needs of
> a great metropolitan area. A medley of scattered and disinte-
> grated local authorities cannot provide the unity required for
> a coherent scheme of development.

How did the Balkanization happen? There is certainly a
historical basis for it. The original colonies and states were
subdivided into counties and townships and widely separated
towns, which with urbanization have grown together. As re-
tired industrialist and author Oscar H. Steiner has so cogently
expressed it:

> The surveyor's instrument of years ago has become a night-
> mare in the twentieth century. The boundaries of the vari-
> ously sized townships, counties and states were drawn at a
> time when the problems we are now confronted with were
> nonexistent and perhaps not even dreamed of. At best, they
> were arbitrary lines. At worst, they were capricious and gerry-
> mandered.

Another who has made the same point is Dr. Luther
Gulick, a leading authority on public administration:

> Our system of local government in America was set up in
> the 1700s and 1800s to fit conditions existing then. And it was
> a marvelous and brilliant invention. But the conditions have
> changed. The living city is no longer within the old city limits.

The problems we are asking local governments to wrestle with now sprawl all over the map.

But it is an error to blame our forefathers for the governmental jungle now smothering our cities. The historic township and county subdivisions pose a relatively smaller problem in metropolitan areas than the more modern incorporated towns, districts and authorities.

The autonomous school district is a phenomenon of the last half of the nineteenth century and the early part of the twentieth. The school district was created to divorce education from the often corrupt influences of politics. By leaving education to educators and public-spirited laymen, we relieved schools of the burden of nepotism and favoritism. School systems levied their own taxes, recruited their teachers and administrators, built their own buildings and sailed the seas of home rule.

For decades this brilliant concept worked superbly. Our excellent system of public education results in large measure from the benefits of home rule. But time and change undermined the system. Americans began the second half of the twentieth century with a welter of small school districts, many of them too poor to afford the modern buildings, laboratories and other facilities of education. Many districts were too small and the wasteful overlapping of services was a disgrace. The solution was consolidation. Small schools were combined into larger ones, particularly at the junior and senior high-school level. During the 1940s and 1950s consolidations took place, but not easily. Local residents fought for their schools, but state governments forced the consolidations as the only way to improve the quality of education.

Consolidation may have occurred, but the school district remains as a separate governmental unit. The school board raises taxes, prepares a budget and manages the affairs of education. Even in those places where the school board does not have separate taxing authority, but depends upon the city or county for funds, the operation of the school system remains autonomous. It is traditional in our country for city officials to keep "hands off" the school system.

This has advantages. Political considerations are minimized. Public-spirited individuals dedicated to education and trained in the conduct of it give undivided attention to its problems. But in the entire context of a city's problems, autonomous education poses difficulties. For example, when a city formulates urban-renewal plans to rebuild and rehabilitate a blighted neighborhood, the quality of the schools is an important consideration. The urban-renewal scheme will certainly call for a new school, but including it in the plan involves negotiations with another government agency, which has its own budget, plans and ideas. In the past, urban-renewal programs have been worked out between city planners and educators, but the process is complex.

An even more difficult problem involves the schools and race relations. City leaders may want to relieve racial tensions by rearranging school districts and transporting pupils to achieve more school desegregation. But plans for this run into the hegemony of individual school districts. The attitudes of local boards may take preference over the larger needs of race relations in the metropolitan area.

Even more debilitating to urban government are the special districts and authorities. Most of these were created as financing mechanisms. Rather than build a bridge, tunnel, highway, sewer or water system out of general tax revenues or burden the credit of the city or state, the special authority was created. A commission was established to operate the facility. It sold bonds to finance the project, and the tolls from the bridge, tunnel or highway, the water and sewer fees, the charges collected at the port or air terminal were reserved for the use of the commission to pay off the bondholders and to maintain and improve the facility. Thus, a whole new governmental unit was established. The city or state government has virtually no control over it.

The public which approved the creation of these authorities had the notion that, when the bridge or tunnel was paid for, the authority would cease to exist. But in practice none of them ever goes out of business. Amortization of the bonds takes decades. Long before that magic day arrives, the authority has sold new bonds to finance improvements, build a new bridge or highway. These authorities are self-perpetuating.

Thus, we have in our metropolitan areas an array of autonomous authorities responsible not to the people or any elected officials, but to the holders of its bonds. The authority has a guaranteed source of income which cannot be touched by any other government agency. In New York City, the Triborough Bridge and Tunnel Authority has a large surplus of funds at a time when the city administration desperately needs money for traffic and transit.

The authority is a new creation for which our forefathers should not be blamed. The incorporated town is a historic device, but our ancestors never made the use of it we moderns do. The framers of our incorporation laws never intended that the City of Beverly Hills should exist as an island entirely surrounded by the City of Los Angeles. It was never envisioned that Cleveland Heights should exist as a separate city on the borders of Cleveland or that Cicero should maintain itself as a separate entity on the edge of Chicago—and there are tens of thousands of examples and more towns are incorporating almost daily.

Why do residents of a suburban area incorporate? Local pride and a desire to keep their residential identity are among the better reasons. A wish to be responsible for the conduct of local affairs is certainly a consideration. But there is also greed. At least in some states, when a town incorporates it shares state gas-tax monies and motor-vehicle license fees. These can be used to repair *local* roads. If people living in another part of the metropolitan area have greater need for this money, that's their problem. When a town incorporates, it sets up its own court system and, in many states, that means it can levy its own traffic fines and keep the money.

The biggest reason for incorporation is fear. If residents of an area are unincorporated, they are subject to the laws of the county to which they belong or risk annexation by a neighboring town. By incorporating, the residents can keep their tax rate low by neglecting "municipal" functions such as schools, highways, police. They can exempt themselves from zoning laws and either keep factories out or allow them to exist contrary to zoning principles. They can make their own building codes, health laws and regulations governing gambling, horse racing and prohibition. As residents of an incorporated town, they can often exempt themselves from smoke-abatement regulations. They won't have to pay for the expensive housing, crime prevention and traffic-control activities of the central city. They are a tight little island divorced from the cares and worries of city dwellers.

Only they aren't. The traffic snarls of the central city ensnare them. The crime reaches out into their homes. The air they breathe becomes polluted, and the shortage of water affects them. The quality of their education, police and fire protection, recreation and all the other services which make for a good city are affected because they are going it alone. To paraphrase the poet John Donne, no incorporated suburb is an island unto itself.

The result of our jungle of metropolitan-area governments is strangulation. Not one problem can be approached on a systematic basis. To solve air-pollution problems in New York, hundreds of individual towns would have to agree to smoke-abatement laws and enforce them equally well. In order to build an adequate highway and mass-transit system, hundreds of towns would need to agree on the routes of these facilities and share in the cost and operation of them. The housing problem may be worse in the central city, but the blighted areas often extend into suburban towns, and the residents uprooted by a slum-clearance project will certainly move into the sacrosanct suburbs. But without intergovernmental cooperation no concerted attack on the problem can be attempted.

The plight of our cities results not so much from ignorance and apathy, not so much from the absence of men of good will determined to solve the problems, as from the sheer impossibility of approaching solutions on a metropolitan-area basis. So many mayors and boards have to be consulted, so many agreements and appropriations have to be approved that the task remains unapproachable. Even when the tasks are undertaken, one community fails to agree and the whole plan has to be abandoned.

In addition to strangulation there is waste. Each city and town puts up traffic lights unmindful of the overall flow of traffic through the area. Intersections that are fatal to life are left untouched, while speed traps are placed on straightaways to ensnare the unwary. Tasks of garbage collection, zoning appeals, building inspection, highway maintenance, police and fire protection and many others that could benefit from centralized administration are duplicated scores of times in town after town. Inefficient services and waste of tax resources result.

Every observer of urban problems has denounced the Balkanization of our metropolitan-area governments. The problem is what to do about it.

One obvious solution is to disband all of the existing towns, counties, and boards and form a super-metropolitan government. There are two difficulties with such a scheme. First, it will never happen. Even if all the incorporated towns and school boards were willing to put themselves out of business —which is unthinkable—that would still not solve the problem. The authorities which represent bondholders could not be disbanded unless the city or state paid off all the bonds, the cost of which would be staggering. But even if that were done, it would not be enough, for many of our metropolitan areas cross state lines. It is pure fantasy to imagine that New Jersey would turn over control of the Newark area to New York and the Camden area to Philadelphia. The city of Cincinnati reaches into Kentucky and Indiana. Chicago reaches into Indiana, Kansas City into Kansas, St. Louis into Illinois, Louisville into Indiana. Tampering with state boundaries to create super cities will never happen.

The second reason some form of super-metropolitan government is unlikely is that the immense municipal administrations would probably be too unwieldy to be efficient. New York City is finding it hard to govern just 7 million people. Mayor John V. Lindsay has set up little city halls throughout the city to bring government closer to the people. Political scientists have long maintained there is a point at which government becomes so large it hamstrings itself.

There are some advantages to our present multiplicity of governments. City hall is relatively close to the people. Public opinion can more easily influence the decisions of government. The routine administration of community affairs can be conducted at neighborhood levels. For example, if a suburban community wants to erect Christmas decorations, it seems senseless to apply to a city administration miles away.

It is only in certain matters affecting the whole metropolitan area that the Balkanization causes troubles. These include highways, traffic, mass transit, air pollution, water and sewage services, taxation and, to a lesser extent, police and fire services, housing, health and recreation.

One proposed solution is some type of partial metropolitan government. Each of the subgovernments would remain, but the metropolitan government would have responsibility for certain functions. Planning would be a metropolitan function. A regional body would be responsible for planning highways, recreation facilities, slum clearance and other projects throughout the area. This would ensure continuity of action and a sensible system of priorities.

Highways, traffic control and mass transit are a must for metropolitan government. Air pollution, water and sewage are concerns for everyone living in the area. Individual communities ought to surrender their autonomy in these matters.

Certain other functions would require less centralized control. Many experts believe that police protection would benefit from more intergovernmental cooperation. Radio communications and patrol facilities could be used more advantageously. The adoption of computers in crime prevention and detection seems to dictate a more unified approach. Common training academies for policemen and firemen are advocated, also. But all of this amounts to cooperation, not amalgamation. Unifying all police and fire departments would probably be too unwieldy to be practical.

Many public administrators have advocated a breakdown of school districts so that schools in one town could handle students from another, but again cooperation, not unification seems to be the goal. Large city school systems have become so complex already that their administration is inefficient.

Several attempts at metropolitan government have been tried. In Canada the Ontario Legislature created the Metropolitan Toronto Corporation in 1953. Originally, it was designed to perform 7 major functions for 13 independent towns, including Toronto: highways, parks, school financing, water and sewer services, certain welfare services, and planning. In 1956, the functions were enlarged to include policing, business licensing and air pollution. The Corporation has no power to tax directly, but assesses each municipality in relation to its share of the area's total property assessment. The Corporation assesses all property to ensure uniformity.

The Toronto plan has been copied in other Canadian cities and is being studied by American cities. It seems to permit a metropolitan attack upon certain problems while allowing each subgovernment to maintain its autonomy.

The Metropolitan District Commission in Boston was established in 1918. It has jurisdiction over water, sewage and parks in the area. It even maintains its own police force in the parks and streets "of a boulevard character."

In Dade County, Florida, which includes Miami and Miami Beach, metropolitan government was voted into being in 1957 to handle such problems as traffic control, zoning, water and sewage, but it has been fought at every turn by many member municipalities. As a result, the metropolitan plan has barely survived repeated attempts to vote it out of existence. The biggest stumbling block has been the attempts to centralize traffic courts. Collection of traffic fines is a major source of revenue in that area. Miami Beach has collected about one million dollars a year, about one third the total collected in the county. It has been most reluctant to lose control over this revenue.

Still another method is used in Houston, where the State of Texas has permitted Houston to reserve most of Harris County for future annexation. Whether such a large city government will be practical remains to be seen, but at least the system eliminates the menace of random incorporation. A similar system has enabled the City of New Orleans to take over the entire Parish of New Orleans.

Perhaps the "cleanest" of the metropolitan-area governments is in Baltimore. The city of Baltimore is a separate political entity and not in a county; thus the State of Maryland consists of 23 counties and Baltimore city. There are no school districts in the state. The schools are operated by the county (and city) governments, but controlled by boards appointed by the mayor and county executives. Most of Baltimore's suburban population resides in Baltimore County, which surrounds Baltimore city on three sides. Baltimore County, despite a population in excess of 600,000 contains no incorporated towns. Government is by the county, which operates on what amounts to a mayor and council system.

As a result of this system, the Baltimore metropolitan area consists of only six governmental jurisdictions, the city and five suburban counties. Historically, the counties have jealously guarded their prerogatives against the city and in many matters cooperation has been nil. Yet it would seem that, with the growing awareness of the need for metropolitan-area cooperation, Baltimore should find the task far easier than most great cities.

There is growing interest throughout the nation in metropolitan-area cooperation. Several states, notably California, have taken steps to make incorporation more difficult and to relieve incorporated towns of some of their powers. Other states, such as Texas and Ohio, have enacted laws to make annexation easier. And city after city, too many to detail here, have begun talks about area cooperation. In some cities, especially New York and Washington, officials from more than one state have been involved.

The federal government has been a goad for this. Urban-renewal and highway funds, among others, have been made available only when they are part of an area or regional plan. This movement was enhanced in 1966 when Congress enacted the Metropolitan Development Act. Under this, the Secretary of Housing and Urban Development is authorized to make supplemental grants to state and local agencies for up to 20 percent of the cost of projects receiving aid under certain other federal programs (such as housing or urban renewal) in metropolitan areas where development is being carried out under metropolitan planning and programming. These supplemental funds—a reward for metropolitan planning—are made available for open spaces, hospitals, libraries, airports, water-supply facilities, sewage treatment plants, transportation, highways and other public-works projects.

There are other provisions of the act, but the intent is clear: to force metropolitan areas to begin cooperating in solution of their problems. This federal attitude comes at a time when many state governments are beginning to aid their cities. Supreme Court decisions in 1962 and 1963 which ordered reapportionment of state legislatures in accordance with the principle of one man–one vote, broke the back of historic rural domination of these bodies. Urban areas are beginning to receive the representation in legislatures commensurate with their population. More aid and support for cities is the inevitable result.

Of greater importance than these governmental changes is the growing awareness of urban residents that their problems can be solved only through metropolitan cooperation. As traffic, crime, welfare costs, air pollution and other problems worsen, old rivalries, greed and fears are giving way to co-operation. Our urban areas are only at the beginnings of metropolitanism. Many difficulties and disappointments lie ahead, but the wave of the future seems headed toward greater metropolitan-area government.

CHAPTER THREE

Too Little Money and No Planning

A "MESS" according to *Webster's New World Dictionary* is "a disorderly or confused collection or mass of things; jumble; hodgepodge; a state of embarrassment, trouble, or difficulty; muddle; a disorderly, untidy or dirty state of things."

Our cities are in a financial mess.

This creaking, much-abused cliché has never been more aptly applied than in reference to urban finances. The cities' jumble of taxes is certainly a hodgepodge. The spending is disorderly and city officials are most definitely embarrassed and in trouble.

There is no more discouraging and disturbing urban problem than the financial impoverishment of our cities. The dilemma is so deeply rooted and has so many facets that, even in moments of greatest optimism, no real solution seems possible. And as long as the financial problem exists so do all the other problems. It may be true that money is not the cure-all for our urban ills, but it is also true that none of the problems can be solved without sufficient funds.

In the summer of 1966, a United States Senate subcommittee headed by Senator Abraham A. Ribicoff of Connecticut held hearings on urban problems. A parade of mayors appeared to discuss their problems. Sooner or later the discussion always got around to money. Mayor John V. Lindsay of New York, a former Congressman, said his city would need 50 billion dollars in federal aid in the next 10 years. The following day Mayor Jerome P. Cavanaugh of Detroit stated a "more modest" figure. The Motor City would need "only"

15 billion dollars in federal aid in the next decade. With that, Senator Robert F. Kennedy of New York computed that America's cities would require 1 trillion dollars—one thousand billion—in federal aid by 1985. And that is on top of state aid and local tax revenues.

Such figures indicate the dimension of the problem, but like all huge combination statistics they are artificial and meaningless. One can state that in 1963–64 the total revenue of U. S. cities was 18.4 billion dollars and that the total expenditure was 19.3 billion dollars. Or, one can point out that the gross debt of local governments in mid-1964 was 68.4 billion dollars, nearly a 400 percent increase in 15 years. During the same period the debt of the federal government increased less than 20 percent.

But even if such figures had meaning other than simple bigness, they would not state the urban financial problem, for the difficulty lies not in what is spent but in what is not spent. In every city, preparation of the annual budget is a crisis. The need for money far, far outstrips available revenues. City budget makers go through an agonizing process, not of trimming expenditures, but of butchering them. Highly desirable programs are curtailed and eliminated. Maintenance appropriations are reduced to a minimum. Salary increases for teachers and civic employees often are postponed, and these people are asked to assume greater workloads. Ultimately, revenues and expenditures are balanced and a make-do budget is concocted. Often the city cannot stick to it. During the year "freezes" are placed on wage increases and the hiring of employees to reduce spending. Sometimes the city has to borrow money to meet operating expenses, as New York did in 1966.

This financial magic has been going on ever since World War II, if not before, and the plight of our cities is the result. An individual or a family can cut back on their expenses when they are in financial difficulty. They can wear last year's clothing, neglect the paint and maintenance on the house, fail to repair appliances, and patch up the car. But such steps can be taken only temporarily. Eventually the clothes, furniture and car wear out and have to be replaced. The house becomes disheveled and deteriorates faster than it would with normal maintenance. Our cities have been "making do" for 20 years and the result is just as predictable—traffic is snarled, school buildings are old, streets are unpaved, mass transit is crippled, water is in short supply and sewage is inadequate. The urban problems being discussed in this book are all seeded in the long-term financial impoverishment of our cities.

Examining the reasons for the cities' financial plight and the possible solutions to it can lead to discouragement.

Many writers on urban affairs discuss the "tax squeeze" of the cities, referring to the fact that many of the upper- and middle-income residents have moved to the suburbs, leaving the city largely populated by low-income residents, who demand more in welfare, health, crime control and other social services. This is a major element in the city's financial plight and will be discussed in detail, but another reason for the financial embarrassment of our cities should be explored.

There are only four major sources of tax revenues for governments. One is a tax on incomes of individuals and corporations. This is the major source of federal revenue. But many states also have income taxes, thus taxing the same income a second time. Some of the states which do not impose an income tax, notably Ohio and Pennsylvania, permit cities and towns to levy a tax on income, frequently calling it an "earnings tax." It amounts to essentially the same thing, however. Inevitably, some cities are beginning to levy a tax on earnings even though there is a state income tax. Thus the residents of New York City are now paying triple income taxes—to city, state and federal governments.

The second major form of revenue is the sales tax. For over a quarter century most states have received the bulk of their revenue from this source. The state places a tax of from 2 to 5 percent on the selling price of merchandise sold or used in the state. (A "use tax" is a levy applied to items bought outside the state but used within the state.) But the federal government also imposes what amounts to sales taxes in the form of excise taxes on luxury items. It also collects import and other custom duties which are reflected in the price of merchandise. This double taxation becomes triple when municipalities impose sales taxes, which is often the case. Sometimes cities collect the sales tax themselves, or the additional pennies charged to a dollar's worth of merchandise are collected by the state and returned to the city. Another form of city sales tax is the gross-receipts tax. The city demands a small portion of the gross receipts of a business—even if the enterprise lost money. This charge is passed on to the consumer.

The third major source of revenue is the property tax, the primary source of local government revenue. Owners of business and residential property pay a tax based upon the assessed value of their land and buildings. In some places, motor vehicles, equipment and even furniture is taxed as property. Most recent estimates are that 87 percent of the local revenues in the United States are derived from property taxes. A fuller discussion of property taxes will follow, but the point now is that state and federal governments also use the tax. Some states apply a direct property tax, but nearly all states, along with the federal government, impose an indirect property tax in the form of inheritance and estate taxes. Certain features of the income tax are a form of property tax in that the income from the sale or use of property is taxed.

The fourth major source of governmental revenue is a conglomeration of levies and charges generally called "nuisance taxes." The term does not mean the taxes are small. Rather, some of the individual taxes produce substantial sums of money and the total revenue from them is immense. The major nuisance taxes, some of which take the form of sales and property taxes, are placed on gasoline and motor vehicles, liquor, cigarettes, all of which are taxed at the federal, state and sometimes local levels; horse racing and other forms of gambling, entertainment, restaurant meals, hotel bills, use of bridges, tunnels and highways. In the nuisance category are a bewildering array of state and local charges and licensing fees for selling liquor, cigarettes and other products, operating an elevator, hanging a sign, erecting a building, parking a car, using city water, sewage or refuse-collection services, holding a parade, attending the civic auditorium or stadium, transferring title to property, getting a traffic ticket. The full list of the ways local governments have thought of to raise money would fill several pages of this book.

The scope of this taxation from cradle to grave is vast. The point here is not to decry that taxation, although the propriety of a 50 percent tax on gasoline, when it is a necessity for most wage earners driving to and from work, seems open to dispute. One of the aims of this discussion is to indicate that our national tax policies are in great need of overhaul. Political scientists have been pointing this out for years.

The most alarming result of our national tax muddle is the impoverishment of cities. This has occurred because, with few exceptions, the biggest, best and most flexible sources of revenue have been denied to the city, namely income and sales taxes. Even when cities have levied these, it has been in desperation, too little and too late at the second and third levels. Similarly, the most lucrative forms of nuisance taxes have been taken over by the state and federal governments, notably gasoline and motor-vehicle, liquor, gambling and cigarette taxes. If the cities have used these taxes, it has been as a small, extra levy.

For the most part, America's urban areas have been left with the property and minor, hard-to-collect nuisance taxes— but state and federal governments also use these. The simple fact is that property and nuisance taxes do not produce enough revenue for cities.

The question is whether the property and nuisance taxes *could* produce enough revenue. They cannot under the present Balkanized metropolitan government. As had been noted, many upper- and middle-income familes fled to the suburbs after World War II. With them went stores and service industries. Shopping centers, drive-ins, gas stations, the whole lexicon of commerce of the American city were erected in the suburbs. Many of these suburban establishments had formerly been located in the central city. Certainly many downtown firms made suburban expansions at the expense of their in-town facilities. Industry, the major source of property-tax revenue, also headed for the suburbs, erecting new plants near suburban expressways.

Many have sought explanations for this movement to the suburbs. A factor certainly was the federal housing program which enabled millions of families to buy homes with small down payments and reasonable interest rates. The Federal Housing Act and home loans for veterans changed the United States from a nation of 52 percent renters to 62 percent homeowners. The automobile, easily purchased on the installment plan, made it easy to buy a home outside the central city where one could have a lawn, trees and flowers. If, subsequently, overcrowded schools, traffic jams and limited recreation facilities became thorns in the suburban bed of roses, the pleasures of homeownership, backyard barbecuing and lawn mowing more than made up for it. Suburban living, as an approximation to the best of both worlds of city dwelling and farm life, seems destined to remain a fixture in our society.

As the middle- and upper-income families left the central city, they were replaced by low-income families arriving from the farms and villages. This phenomenon has been statistized to death. Urban America, Inc., reports that the rural population of the United States has shrunk from 78 percent in 1900 to 33 percent in 1960. Further shrinkage, to 29 percent, is expected by 1980. Between 1940 and 1950 a net total of 7.5 million people left the farms. In the next decade almost 10 million farmers migrated to the urban areas. Lest it be wondered why the urban population hasn't starved to death, the statisticians point out the increased productivity of the surviving farmers. One farmer feeds 33 people today, three times as many as in 1940.

Not everyone left the central city nor did all those who migrated from rural areas settle in downtown areas, but the division between city dweller and suburbanite was determined by income. The center city housing which had been vacated by the new suburbanites— largely because they felt it was not so pleasant and valuable as a home in the greenswards—was occupied by those who could not afford suburban living. Thus, the center city became the domain of the poor, the aged and the Negro, who, even when he could afford suburban living, was denied access to it.

Recent Bureau of Census figures show that 11.6 percent of all American families earn less than 2,000 dollars a year, 20 percent less than 3,000 dollars, and 29 percent less than 4,000 dollars. Thus nearly one third of the families cannot afford to rent a standard three-bedroom house or apartment in most cities. They are forced to settle for part of a house or a one-bedroom "apartment." A house that formerly housed four to seven people may contain twice or three times that many. The wear and tear of overoccupancy speeds deterioration of the property.

In actuality, wear and tear weren't normal. The absentee owner, taking no pride in his property, kept repairs to a minimum, and his attitude was reflected in that of his tenants. And pride comes dear when your family income is less than 2,000 dollars a year. Thus, a deadly spiral was set in operation. Poverty bred overcrowding, which led to deterioration. Still lower-income tenants moved in and more deterioration occurred. In a matter of months sometimes, formerly grand neighborhoods of city townhouses deteriorated into shabby tenements.

The effect of housing deterioration and the flight to the suburbs on the tax coffers of the central city was staggering. For example, between 1930 and 1963 the city of Boston raised its property-tax rate from 31 dollars per thousand dollars of assessment to almost 100 dollars, but at the same time its real-estate valuations declined from 1.8 billion dollars to 1.3 billion dollars. The experience has been repeated in city after city.

At the same time, as its ability to raise revenues from the property tax declined, the city's need for more money increased. The poverty-stricken who were the new residents required more health services, more welfare payments. Sanitation was a bigger problem and fire in the tenements was a greater risk. Crime increased. From 1954 to 1964, America's cities increased expenditures for housing and urban renewal by 132 percent, for education 105 percent, for police 98 percent, for sanitation 87 percent, for health services 90 percent, for fire protection 81 percent, for welfare 87 percent. Current operating expenses doubled. And these efforts were not nearly enough. Housing deterioration continued largely unchecked, along with health, education, crime control and the rest.

It was not alone the poverty of a large segment of its residents that caused the central city's financial woes. Former city residents, now ensconced in the suburbs, still demanded city services. Almost to a man, the suburbanites got into their cars every morning and sought to drive to their places of employment in city offices, factories, stores and banks. City traffic was reduced to one vast snarl, creating a great expense in traffic control, street repaving and expressway building. Suburban residents continued to use city hospitals, city parks, recreation and entertainment facilities, city police and fire protection, if only during working hours. They expected the city library to stay up to date, for it exceeded the usefulness of the inadequate suburban institutions. Then at night the suburbanites got back into their cars, inched through another traffic jam to their havens and paid their taxes to the suburban towns.

If the central city raised tax rates to provide the services demanded of it, the flight to the suburbs by higher-income residents, business and industry intensified, for the suburbs offered the attraction of lower tax rates. That the suburban communities offered fewer services didn't matter, because the middle- and upper-income residents demanded less. They could afford to shift for themselves.

The major thought behind most central city tax policies since World War II has been to find a way to force suburban residents to pay for the city services they use. Charging suburbs for city water and sewage services has become routine. A variety of charges for parking, entertainment, etc., have been invoked. Imposing a city sales tax to ensnare the suburban shopper has been tried. But the principal means of taxing the suburbanite has been the earnings tax, making the suburbanite pay where he works and not where he lives. But all of these methods are insufficient to meet the financial needs of the city.

Returning to the question of whether property and nuisance taxes could be made adequate to urban financial needs, one finds considerable evidence that they could not. Part of the tax squeeze strangling cities is that many of the solutions to urban problems reduce the property-tax base. Thus a new expressway may speed the flow of traffic, but it removes large acreage from the tax rolls. A public-housing project may improve living conditions for the poor, but the project is exempt from property taxes.

A study reported by the Tax Institute, Inc., of Princeton, N. J., showed that, of the developed land in 11 urban areas, 28 percent was used for residences, 2.7 percent for commerce, 2.7 percent for industry and 6.2 percent for railroads, for a total of 42.5 percent. The remaining 57.5 percent was devoted to streets, parks and playgrounds, and other public and semi-public uses, including hospitals, churches, libraries, court houses—and all were tax exempt.

A study by the Urban Land Institute of seven cities showed 35.8 percent of the developed area was in residences, 3.4 percent in commercial establishments and 10.3 percent in railroads and industry. The remaining 50.2 percent of the land was tax exempt. A study in Chicago showed that 59.8 percent of the land was taxable. In New York City, on the other hand, only 39.7 percent of the developed land was taxable.

The trend is definitely toward a shrinking tax base, as the cities continue public-works projects for government buildings, health and educational facilities, airports, mass-transit facilities and housing projects. There is also a reverse trend, as will be shown, toward improving property values by downtown renewal and rehabilitation of deteriorated neighborhoods. At best the two trends cancel each other out, leaving the tax base still inadequate for future needs.

If the property tax, aided by nuisance taxes, seems unlikely to meet the financial needs of urban areas, there is no doubt that improvement could be made. If suburban-area residents paid their fair share to the housing, health, welfare, traffic and other needs of the whole area, rather than enjoying lower taxes in their tax havens, the financial problems could be alleviated. But with the gaggle of incorporated towns and the current laissez-faire attitude of suburbanites, such financial cooperation seems improbable. City mayors are trying another way to accomplish the same ends. They are asking the state and federal governments to collect the money from suburbanites as income and sales taxes and return it to the cities as federal and state appropriations. If the mayors' wishes are granted, city finances will improve. Unfortunately, taxpayers will be one step further removed from control over the spending of their tax money.

There is another aspect to the urban financial mess. Exceptions exist, to be sure, but as a rule urban-area governments are inept, wasteful and inefficient.

The rallying cry of the opponents at the annual budget crisis is "waste in government." The statement is heard over and over that if the city would "cut the fat out of the budget" and eliminate wasteful programs, taxes would not have to be raised and there would be plenty of money for necessary programs.

When I was a newspaper reporter in Baltimore, I participated in several journalistic campaigns to reduce city spending. Over the years the three Baltimore newspapers successfully campaigned for the discontinuation of free public baths, dissolution of the fire department's salvage corps, amalgamation of the park police with the city police, and the junking of two creaking, post-Civil War ice breakers the city maintained even though the Coast Guard performed this function. There were other successes, but, at least by 1964, the journalists had not been successful in eliminating the police mounted unit, disbanding either the police rescue squad or the firemen's rescue squad, which performed the same functions, or persuading the city to drop its requirement that city paving contractors operate two asphalt plants. This requirement guaranteed that one of six paving contractors would get the contract and that the bid would be high.

Every city has had similar experiences with municipal programs that have outlived their initial purposes. While it would be advantageous to eliminate unneeded activities and to make governmental agencies more efficient, that is not where the real waste occurs in city government.

The biggest expense in any government operation—and this is true of commerce and industry as well—is personnel. The costs of hiring, training and paying personnel their salaries, fringe benefits and retirement are greater than the costs of supplying them materials and equipment with which to work. The state and local civil services have grown to immense size, employing 7,200,000 people, compared to 2,400,000 in the federal civil service. Where the federal service has remained fairly stable in size, the state and local services are growing rapidly.

There are many intelligent, talented, resourceful and dedicated people in the local civil service, but, in general, deficiencies exist in both the quality and quantity of the service. Such a statement is difficult to document because there are thousands of separate local services each governed—some well—by their own rules and procedures. But I uncovered some indication of the quantitative problem in Baltimore.

The cost of city government was examined in terms of *people* rather than dollars. The results were both amusing and alarming, as the following items indicate:

The city hired 23 more people to clean and maintain the same City Hall building than it had 10 years previously. Where 173 employees were needed to maintain 10 downtown city buildings a decade before, 216 were needed for the same tasks in only eight buildings.

City Hospitals had 435 more employees, although the number of patients and the "annual patient days" declined markedly.

The case load of the Welfare Department increased 37 percent in the decade, but employment rose 82 percent.

The Department of Building Inspection added 180 men to inspect 4,000 fewer buildings.

The Bureau of Transportation operated 38 percent more vehicles, yet its personnel increased by 238 percent.

School enrollment jumped 49 percent in the decade. The number of teachers kept pace at 52 percent, but the noneducational personnel increased by 97 percent.

There were exceptions, but the pattern of more employees to perform less work was discovered in many agencies.

There is a natural tendency toward increased personnel in almost every governmental and mercantile enterprise. Every executive, from the junior grades up, feels he needs an assistant, secretary, clerk and others to help him. If he had this assistance he could do a better job, as well as qualify for a higher salary. Empire building is a long-observed human tendency. At the same time there is political pressure to add supporters and their relatives and friends to the payroll. Perhaps the biggest personnel booster is the fact that municipal programs seldom go out of business. The service may decline in popularity, but the personnel remain.

Leaders of municipal civil services are well aware that civic operations would benefit from efficiency studies. In these, the activities of every employee are examined to discover precisely what he does during the day. Overlapping duties are separated. But such studies are time-consuming and expensive. Most urban personnel departments cannot afford them, so the inefficient, top-heavy personnel practices remain.

If our urban areas are to achieve the greatness they desire, they will have to improve the quality of their civil services. Cities need to hire better men and women, pay them higher salaries and offer them genuine career advancement.

The federal civil service is a model to be emulated in these tasks. In the last decade, truly amazing improvements have been made in the federal civil service. Salaries were increased to levels competitive with and sometimes exceeding those offered by industry. Rules were changed so that new, highly-trained employees could be recruited at higher levels. More importantly, the pay scales of the middle and upper levels were increased sharply. A scientist, engineer or technician may join the federal civil service at a salary somewhat lower than he can earn in private industry, but in a few years he can earn promotions on the basis of merit to positions paying in excess of 20,000 dollars a year. Salaries of 12,000 dollars to 15,000 dollars are common. Nor does the employee need to become a supervisor to reach these salaries. He is promoted because he is valuable in the work he is doing.

Perhaps the most significant action taken by the United States Civil Service Commission to improve the federal civil service has been its policy of unlimited transfer. Any employee of the government can move at will to another government agency. He simply applies for a job in another agency that is more interesting, challenging, higher paid and offers greater advancement. If accepted for this post, his former supervisor cannot keep him from going to the new job, no matter how valuable he may be. As a result of this policy, able, ambitious Federal employees are able to "shift for themselves," plan and develop careers, avoid "dead-end" jobs, and eliminate dull, uninspiring work—while maintaining their overall retirement and fringe benefits.

In comparison, a study I made of the New York City Civil Service, second in size to the federal civil service, showed that, while starting salaries were often higher, middle and upper earnings were much lower. Intragovernment transfer was extremely difficult. Thus, the New York civil service, by its policies, rewards the inexperienced employee while stifling the incentives and opportunities for careers in municipal service. It would appear that New York, and perhaps other cities, could improve their personnel and the quality of government by methods no more difficult than simple procedural changes.

One aspect of municipal government in particular need of improvement is planning. This subject will be discussed repeatedly in chapters to follow, but at this point the stepchild nature of urban planning should be mentioned.

The planning function encompasses a broad spectrum of activities, including zoning, building codes, land use, architecture, beautification. With good planning, a city can ensure orderly growth and development. Industry can be placed to have access to highways and railroads and where its smoke and noise and traffic do not blight residential neighborhoods. Commercial establishments can be located, not only in relation to highways, but in conjunction with appropriate residential areas. Planning can ensure that upper-, middle- and low-income housing is related to appropriate services, that parks, playgrounds and open spaces relieve the monotony of the urban vista, that buildings are not only well constructed but architecturally satisfying. In a word, planning means order instead of chaos. The industrial, commercial and residential uses of land are related to transportation and the needs and desires of the people living and working there.

The lack of planning scars our cities. The world's largest commercial office building, housing thousands of workers, is erected in New York with parking for 200 cars. Housing developments are built next to truck routes, railroads and airports. Seashores and lake fronts are snapped up for private use and public access is denied. Luxury stores are opened in low-income areas. High-rise apartments are erected on crowded city streets far from the nearest expressway. Factories are built in residential areas.

"There isn't a metropolitan area in the U. S. that has a comprehensive plan to accommodate its growth," says Baltimore developer James W. Rouse. "The best prospect we have is that we will become a nation of Los Angeleses." That West Coast metropolis is often called "17 suburbs in search of a city," although the number of suburbs now exceeds 75. The flippancy is intended to convey that Los Angeles lacks a downtown, a central core that unifies the urban area. Towns and suburbs grew any way they wanted. But Los Angeles is far from unique. Houston became a major city without any zoning at all.

Planning has always been suspect in cities. The planner has been looked upon as an impractical individual residing in an ivory tower, divorced from the exigencies of everyday life. Granted that planners sometimes talk "another language" and that their plans sometimes fail to differentiate between the desirable and the possible, but the stereotype of the planner is grossly incorrect. The urban planner is usually right in his views. If he had been listened to over the years, many of the problems being faced today would not exist.

He was not heard because his plan demanded regimentation. A builder would far rather erect any sort of cheap and unsightly structure in whatever location he wished than conform to an orderly pattern of architectural controls and land use. It was far more profitable to build a lot of small houses jammed together than to leave space for lawns or an area vacant for a playground. The temptation was always to build the housing development and let the "other fellow" worry about the schools and the shopping center, and let the city worry about the traffic problems, the office building or apartment house, and let the "powers that be" figure where the cars were to be parked.

By sheer necessity—and federal insistence—this attitude is disappearing. But urban planning has a long way to go. As has been noted, planning must be done on a metropolitan-area basis. Competent planners must be recruited to work in an atmosphere free from political pressure. When the comprehensive urban-area plan is developed, it must be explained to residents, approved and voted into law. Then, it must be enforced so that henceforth all building and other developments conform to the plan. Exceptions to the plan based on political expediency must be eliminated.

None of this is easy. The regimentation imposed by the plan is foreign to our heritage of individual choice and free enterprise. The plan must be flexible, of course, but it must have integrity. In our urban problems we see the chaos that results from failure to plan.

CHAPTER FOUR

The Urban Ghetto

URBAN PROBLEMS have somehow become racial problems. Lack of mass transit facilities and absence of a nearby hospital were major factors in the 1965 riot in the Watts area of Los Angeles. Rioting continued for four to five days. Thirty-five were killed, 947 injured and property damage was estimated at 40 million dollars. Wretched housing, gross poverty and despair were prime factors in similar riots in the Hough area of Cleveland in 1966. The even more violent 1967 riots, particularly those which laid waste large areas of Detroit and Newark, were seeded in the same factors.

It could be argued that poverty, poor housing, inadequate transportation and health facilities have no relationship to the color of a man's skin. People of all races and persuasions are affected by these and similar difficulties. Statistics could be cited to show our urban problems are problems of the aged, for example.

But the fact remains that, because the central cities of our major urban areas have such a large percentage of Negroes, nonracial urban problems have become identified in the minds of many people as racial problems.

The Negro population of cities is large and growing rapidly. The following table shows in percentages the size of the Negro population of major cities in 1960 and estimates for the year 2000:

City	Percent Negro in 1960	Percent Negro in 2000
Washington, D. C.	53.9	75
Cleveland	28.6	67
Newark, N. J.	34.1	63
Baltimore	34.7	56
Chicago	22.9	55
New York	14.0	50
Philadelphia	26.4	50
Detroit	28.9	50
St. Louis	28.6	50
Atlanta	38.3	44
Kansas City	17.5	42
Cincinnati	21.6	40
San Francisco–Oakland	14.3	40
Houston	22.9	34
Buffalo	13.3	34
Pittsburgh	16.7	34
Paterson–Clifton–Passaic, N. J.	9.3	34
Boston	9.1	31
Dallas	19.0	30
Milwaukee	8.4	29
Los Angeles	12.2	20

These are census figures and estimates primarily for central cities. Suburban Negro populations are also expected to increase, but to a lesser degree:

Suburbs of	Percent Negro in 1960	Percent Negro in 2000
San Francisco–Oakland	4.8	22
Washington, D. C.	6.1	19
Baltimore	6.7	19
Philadelphia	6.1	18
Detroit	3.7	13
Houston	10.3	12
Cincinnati	3.4	12
Cleveland	.7	12
Newark	6.7	10
Chicago	2.9	10
San Diego	1.1	10

All other major city suburbs will be less than 10 percent Negro by 2000, although considerable growth is expected to occur.

The estimates of the Negro population at the end of the century, prepared by *U. S. News and World Report*, assume that present birthrates, population growth and other trends will continue. But there is evidence these trends will not continue. An assumption that Negro Americans will not undergo drastic economic change and thereby social change in the next one-third century seems unwarranted.

The 1960 figures are real. They show a large Negro population in most of our major central cities. When other statistics are added, a picture of the plight of urban Negro Americans emerges. In 1964 almost 30 percent of the nonwhite males in the U. S. were unemployed during some part of the year, almost half of them 14 weeks or longer—and this figure has held fairly constant since 1940. The income of nonwhite families is slightly more than half that of white families. Nonwhite families with incomes of less than 2,000 dollars a year average two more children than nonwhite families earning 7,000 dollars or more a year. Recent statistics show that 56 percent of Negro children receive Aid for Dependent Children, a form of welfare subsistence, sometime during the year, compared to 8 percent of white children. A study in Philadelphia showed that only 5 percent of Negroes could afford to purchase a 12,000-dollar home even under the most liberal credit terms.

Such statistics have value, but they do not tell the full story. For example, the number of Negro college students has doubled in 20 years to 300,000. Individual incomes for Negro rose 54 percent from 1950 to 1960. Family income increased 73 percent in that period. In 1961, 20 percent of all Negro families made more than 6,000 dollars a year, compared to only 4 percent in 1945. The percentage of Negroes living in standard housing doubled from 1950 to 1960. The number of Negroes employed rose from 6,721,000 in 1957 to 7,747,000 in 1966, with the civil service accounting for most of the increase. Negro employment in the professional and technical fields increased 130 percent in a decade.

The deficiency of all such computations is that they lump all Negro Americans into one group when, in fact, there are many groups. Thus, the statistics do not reflect the accurate situation in any group. There are Negro millionaires whose income figures are extremely high. The "averages" do not reflect the true situation among the Negro middle class, and they do not correctly portray the wretched poverty of the lowest-income Negroes.

White people have a regrettable tendency to combine all Negroes together, ignoring the fact that perhaps as many as 40 percent of all Negroes are in the middle class, with representative incomes and stable families. Most of the economic and social gains earned and won by Negroes in the last two decades have benefited the Negro middle class and both the numbers and percentage of Negroes reaching that economic strata have grown markedly.

In 1966, *Newsweek* magazine polled Negroes on their attitudes toward gains that have been made in certain areas and compared the results to a similar poll in 1963. Fifty-four percent said they had more satisfaction in their work, compared to 45 percent in 1963. Fifty-five percent found it easier to use public accommodations, compared to 35 percent three years previously. Fifty-eight percent, compared to 39 percent in 1963, felt school integration was better, and 53 percent declared it was easier to register and vote, as against only 31 percent in the earlier poll.

One area where no improvement was noted was housing. In both surveys, 45 percent thought housing accommodations had improved. This survey indicates that, while the Negro middle class is enjoying improvement in employment, education and public accommodations, it is still experiencing segregated housing. Outside the South, Negroes and whites are probably more segregated today than ever before. Many white upper-, middle- and upper-lower classes moved to the suburbs, physically removing themselves from the inner-city areas largely populated by Negroes. Four out of five Negro children attend schools that are virtually all black. In 1957 there were 64 schools in New York City that were 90 percent or more Negro or Puerto Rican. Six years later the number of such schools was 134.

It seems inevitable that middle-class Negroes will break out of the segregated housing pattern. Open occupancy in housing is perhaps first on the list of goals of Negro civil-rights leaders. As the Negro vote makes itself increasingly felt in city councils and state legislatures, passage of open-housing laws seems assured. But such laws and policies will not desegregate housing. The federal government has had open-housing rules for federally financed housing for some time, but no great migration of Negroes to such developments has occurred. White intransigence to Negro neighbors is certainly a factor, but it seems more likely that lack of the necessary financial wherewithal has kept the Negro segregated. As job discrimination declines—and it has a lot of declining to do—and the financial resources of Negroes improve, it seems inevitable that middle-class Negroes will enjoy the lure of the suburbs. That patch of lawn and a flower bed are more of an attraction for the Negro, long contained in dreary city blocks, than they were for his white suburban predecessors. Middle-class Negro Americans may still be segregated in the suburbs, but in the suburbs they will *be*.

White Americans living in the suburbs who have not ventured through Negro areas of the city for years often have the mistaken notion that all Negroes live in ghettos, as the slums have come to be called. They do not. Nor are all Negro residential areas blighted. Eunice S. Grier of the Washington Center for Metropolitan Studies observed:

> Huge areas of Washington have changed from white to Negro in a brief 10 years. Some of Washington's finest neighborhoods have changed. They remain fine neighborhoods today—with imposing stone and brick houses set far back on beautifully landscaped and immaculately maintained lawns. But the children playing in those yards today are Negro,

whereas a few years ago they were white. The women waving goodbye to their husbands as they drive off to work are all Negro. . . . A fact that strikes the observer with great force is that the houses and the general flavor of the neighborhoods have changed little or none. But the color of the inhabitants has changed completely.

This quotation has been included because it conveys the quality and attractiveness of middle-class Negro neighborhoods, but it is regrettable that the author had to be struck "with great force" that this was so. What did she expect? The proverbial coal in the bathtub?

If the Negro middle class is growing and beginning to grasp the opportunity for equality which is the birthright of all Americans, the plight of the lower-class Negro in the urban ghetto is worsening. These are the most downtrodden of the downtrodden, rock bottom on our economic and social scale. They are victims both of white prejudice and Negro hostility. The middle-class Negro, who is beginning to gain some of the fruits of American society, sees the ghetto Negro as a drag on his progress. The white man lumps all Negroes together and applies his image of the Negro slum dweller to all Negroes. The educated, responsible Negro has to combat this image and may feel hostile to the lower-class Negro who is the subject of the image.

It is conditions in the ghetto, not those of middle-class Negro neighborhoods, that have been identified with urban problems. And, it must be noted that not all ghettos are Negro. New York, for example, has a large Puerto Rican population living under much the same conditions as the ghetto Negro. Housing is blighted, welfare costs are high, crime is common, poverty is the order of the day, a riot seems only an incident away. Sanitation and health conditions are below standard, education is below normal and drug addiction is beyond belief.

The social and economic problems of the ghetto dwellers are the most complex and severe our country has ever faced. There is universal poverty, with much of it of the abject variety wherein financial resources do not keep a roof over the head, food on the table and clothes on the back. For many there is little hope of doing anything about the poverty, for they do not have the means of earning a living. They have settled to this low state because they have been so denied opportunities for education and training that they are unemployable. They have few marketable occupational skills to offer employers in this automated age. There are only so many menial jobs available and a glut of people to fill them. The craft labor unions have remained militantly segregated, thus keeping a door closed to Negroes on a passageway to the middle class which comparable white youths have used for generations. A white youth who drops out of school but has manual dexterity can go into craft work, but the similar Negro finds it grossly difficult.

The Negro male from deep in the ghetto who goes job hunting finds obstacles at every turn. His skin is black, he has no marketable skills, he is a school dropout and his employment record is spotty at best. He can't afford presentable clothes, his attitude is something less than optimistic and the polished manners and urbane chatter of the white man's world are foreign to his ghetto origins. Working his way out of the ghetto is a superhuman task.

Poverty begets poverty and, when poverty persists generation after generation, as it has in the ghetto, it causes a profound social change. All of a sudden "everyone" is observing the change and the statistics spew out in a flood. Thirty-six percent of Negro children are living in broken homes at any specific moment. Nearly one quarter of Negro women living in cities who have ever married are divorced, separated or living apart from their husbands. Nearly one quarter of Negro births are illegitimate, almost eight times the white ratio. Almost one fourth of nonwhite families are headed by a woman. The average Negro male has three years less schooling than his white counterpart. Fifty-seven percent of eighteen- and nineteen-year-old Negro males are one or more years behind in their schooling. One third of all youths in training schools for delinquents are Negro. Three out of five persons arrested for major crimes in cities are Negroes. Four times as many Negroes as whites fail the Armed Forces mental tests. Narcotics addiction in Harlem is eight times that of New York City as a whole. In a recent year, Negroes composed 54 percent of the addict population in the United States.

These figures must be read with a suspicious eye. Very often nonwhite statistics—including Indians, Chinese and Japanese, almost 10 percent of the total nonwhite population —are quoted as Negro statistics. More importantly, these figures do not give an accurate picture of the Negro middle class, whose family and social life is just as stable as that of the white middle class. One can only conclude that, if actual statistics were drawn for all ghetto residents, they would be even more alarming than these.

But even these statistics, if they existed, would only measure the problems. They would in no way explain them. Every scientific inquiry has shown that the Negro is in no way different, let alone inferior, to other races. So what factors can account for the high incidence of unemployment, crime and addiction, the observed breakdown in family life and the measured reduction in intelligence scores?

The consensus of reputable scholars is that observed and measured differences are the product of poverty, prejudice and the cultural and social influences of the ghetto. Many studies have shown that environment affects intelligence. A child who grows up in a home where books are read, knowledge is esteemed, and conversation is intellectually stimulating will register higher on IQ tests. Similarly, IQ scores[1] will be depressed when the child's environment is not intellectually stimulating, when his vocabulary is limited and when scholarship does not earn him particular social prestige. Other factors contributing to poor school performance, which

[1] It has been pointed out often that the IQ tests themselves are tailored to the white middle-class person and do not fairly measure the Negro and other minority groups.

in itself lowers IQ scores, will be discussed in Chapter 8. The point here is that a welter of environmental influences in the ghetto depress intelligence and mar school performance. The resultant lack of education, plus the long-standing prejudice of employers, contribute to unemployment. The idleness, futility and despair of unemployment lead, in a vicious circle, to crime, drug addiction and other activities which worsen the environment. These factors will be discussed in Chapter 9.

Another result of ghetto environment is its adverse effect on family life. It is perhaps impossible for any man, white or black, who has never experienced the ghetto to understand the way of life created by prolonged poverty. A man who is chronically unemployed and probably unemployable cannot support a family, so why try? Psychologists and sociologists have long pointed out that poverty and financial worries are the most destructive forces in marriage. They pose strains on even the most loving and stable marital relationship.

This breakdown in family structure is further encouraged by federal welfare programs, which Professor Daniel P. Moynihan, former assistant secretary of labor, called "a form of social insanity." Aid for Dependent Children is given to indigent children *only* when the father has died, is disabled or has deserted his wife and children. Thus only the broken family can receive this aid. When the father is out of work, his family will be better off financially if he deserts than if he stays in the home. The family that stays together in time of adversity is thus penalized. True, since 1961 there are allowances to unemployed men, but these represent only 10 percent of the AFDC cases. No other major, industrialized nation fails to provide aid to families before they break up.

The AFDC system does more than encourage family breakup. It virtually begs fraud. The musical comedy, *Golden Boy*, had a scene in which Negro racketeers in Harlem were calling upon women in the neighborhood collecting payments. This referred to the practice wherein a man allows himself to be named the father of several illegitimate children in return for a portion of the welfare checks paid to the mothers.

In order to qualify for the AFDC aid, a mother must swear out a warrant with the police department for the arrest of her deserted husband. Often, perhaps most often, this is a legitimate warrant. But some of the time it is not. The father of her children has left the home, but she knows where he is. He may secretly continue to take some meals in the home and spend a few nights there. Some years ago the Baltimore Department of Welfare set up a special squad of detectives to investigate welfare fraud. They would visit homes at odd hours of the day and night. If a man was found asleep or to have some clothing or other evidence of residence—not just the father, but any man—the woman was taken off welfare. This eventually led to several dozen prosecutions for welfare fraud.

Simple humanity dictates the conclusion that, if fault must be found, it is in the welfare system and not in the individuals involved.

The pernicious influence of poverty in the ghetto not only encourages breakup of the family, it precludes the formation of it. Love and marriage may go together in the middle classes, but in the white and Negro ghetto, marriage is an economic luxury, while love is a necessity in the dull, desolate, despairing world of poverty. Love offers warmth and tenderness, encouragement and companionship in a cruel existence. In a society where intellectual attainments, wealth, possessions, power, success and all the ways middle-class Negroes and whites gain recognition and response from others are so hard to find, physical attractiveness offers both recognition and, certainly, response. In this way occurs one of the strangest phenomena of the ghetto. Unlike middle-class people who are ashamed of an illegitimate child and hide the fact by juggling birth records or placing the child for adoption, ghetto women often take pride in their children. Thus, an unwed ghetto mother asked the married, college-educated, well-bred welfare worker, "How many children do you have?" When the case worker said she had none, the girl replied, "I'm more of a woman than you are." Having illegitimate children by more than one man is to some a badge of merit. The children keep the last names of their respective fathers, and the fathers take pride in their children. Even if they have children by several women, they will proudly claim them, take some role in their upbringing and do their level best to provide gifts for them at Christmas and on birthdays. This has long been observed in domestic-relations courts. Fathers from the ghetto tend to miss their December support payments because they are buying presents for their children.

Such ghetto situations are far, far from universal, but they do occur. Perhaps some will think these are not matters to be discussed in a book for young people, yet these social mores are the problems to be solved by young people in the years to come.

A court probation department in a large Eastern city prepared some case histories for me which illuminate the social and family problems of the ghetto.

Case One

This first came to the probation department in 1928 when a woman, herself an illegitimate child, brought a complaint against one of the three men who had fathered her three out-of-wedlock children. She then married and had six legitimate children. After leaving her husband, she had two more illegitimate children by another man. Her husband went on to have one other child who became a probation case.

Of this woman's 11 children:

No. 1—Himself an illegitimate, he became a probation case when he failed to support his wife.

No. 2—He married and had five children. Later he had two children out of wedlock by a woman who had four illegitimate children by three different men. No. 2 moved to another city, where he fathered additional illegitimate offspring.

No. 3—This son is without a probation record.

No. 4—This girl married and was divorced. There were no children of the union, but she subsequently had two illegitimate children by two men. Her divorced husband meanwhile had two children by another woman who had four legitimate children. Her divorced husband has a child born out of wedlock by still another woman.

No. 5—No probation record for this girl.

No. 6—This girl had four illegitimate children by four men, one of whom has one other child by a woman having three others.

No. 7—His probation record shows a nonsupport complaint by his wife and five children. The wife had one other illegitimate offspring.

No. 8—He is the father of one out-of-wedlock child.

No. 9—This daughter has two illegitimate children by two men.

No. 10—This illegitimate child has two herself by two men.

No. 11—This boy is still a teenager.

This case reflects four generations of illegitimacy. Altogether 35 illegitimate and 16 legitimate children are involved. Nearly all the family have been on welfare for three generations. Several of the children are in foster care. At least two of the men and two of the women have been imprisoned.

Case Two

This man married and divorced. There were no children. Then he lived with another woman, three illegitimate children resulting. This second woman has three other illegitimate children. The man lived with a third woman and fathered two more children by the woman, who has two legitimate children. The man now lives with a fourth woman, who has two children born out of wedlock.

Case Three

This woman had one illegitimate child by one man; a second child by another man sought by police; two children by a third man; and three children by a fourth man. She has never married.

Case Four

This man in single. He has lived with a woman off and on for 12 years, resulting in 11 children, 10 living. The woman has another child by a man she never married. In addition to the 10 by the one woman, the man has fathered two children by a second woman. To support all 12 children, he pays 22 dollars a week through the Probation Department. He earns 50 dollars a week.

Case Five

This man first had three illegitimate children by woman No. 1. Then he married another woman and had three more children. Later, he had twins by No. 1. Still later he had three more children by his wife. Then he had another child by No. 1. He is unemployed.

Absolutely no moral judgment should be made of these cases or the people involved except by those who have experienced ghetto poverty as did their parents and grandparents. We have the opinion of Arthur Dunmeyer in testimony before the Senate subcommittee chaired by Senator Abraham A. Ribicoff of Connecticut. Mr. Dunmeyer, himself an illegitimate child, has eight children, including a daughter who bore an illegitimate child at the age of twelve. "It's our way of life," he testified. "We have just so many ways to express ourselves. You have a girl, a mother, a friend." Mr. Dunmeyer said his mother "had to scratch for a living, she had to hold on, she had to eat before she fed me. To others she was a prostitute. But to this day, I respect her for not bowing down."

Mr. Dunmeyer and his friend, author Claude Brown, who rose from the ghetto to write a best-selling book about his childhood experiences, *Manchild in the Promised Land,* described life in the ghetto and the values of the residents. The idol of the ghetto, Mr. Brown told the subcommittee, is not the soldier in uniform or the cop on the beat or the politician sitting at a big desk. "It's the man in the 200-dollar silk suit. He's the real soldier. He's the general. He's winning the war, and if he gets busted, he's just a prisoner of war."

By the man in the silk suit, Mr. Brown was referring to the racketeer operating the numbers game. "If you can't get downtown and get the big stack, you take the little stack uptown," Mr. Dunmeyer said. "I never thought it was wrong." He added, "You're in jail, whether you're in the streets or behind bars."

The testimony of the two men moved Senator Robert F. Kennedy of New York to say, "We give our money and go back to our homes and maybe our swimming pools and wonder, 'Why don't they keep quiet? Why don't they go away?' " Senator Ribicoff commented, "This gap between government and the people—we seem to be talking about two different worlds."

Indeed we are.

Several efforts have been made to explain the values of the Negro ghetto in terms of the history of slavery in this country.

Nathan Glazer has described slave conditions in these terms:

> The slave was totally removed from the protection of organized society (compare the elaborate provisions for the protection of slaves in the Bible), his existence as a human being was given no recognition by any religious or secular agency, he was totally ignorant of and completely cut off from his past, and he was offered absolutely no hope for the future. His children could be sold, his marriage was not recognized, his wife could be violated or sold (there was something comic about calling the woman with whom the master

permitted him to live a "wife"), and he could also be subject, without redress, to frightful barbarities—there were presumably as many sadists among slaveowners, men and women, as there are in other groups. The slave could not, by law, be taught to read or write; he could not practice any religion without the permission of his master, and he could never meet with his fellows for religious or any other purposes, except in the presence of a white; and finally, if a master wished to free him, every legal obstacle was used to thwart such action.

Glazer points out that this was the "most awful" form of slavery in the world, vastly more dehumanizing than that practiced in Latin America.

Many scholars feel the roots of the Negro ghetto mores are in slavery, where family life was not just discouraged, but forbidden. But others contend such an explanation is incorrect. The middle-class Negroes and the lower-class Negroes who enjoy a stable family life are just as close or far from slavery as the others. Dr. Elizabeth Herzog, chief of the Child Life Studies Branch, Children's Bureau, Welfare Administration, U. S. Department of Health, Education, and Welfare, has pointed out:

> Descriptions of white families at the very low-income levels read very much like current descriptions of poor Negro families, with high incidence of broken homes, "mother dominance," births out of wedlock, educational deficit, crowded living, three-generation households, and failure to observe the norms of middle-class behavior.

Thomas F. Pettigrew, writing in *A Profile of the Negro American* (Princeton, N. J.: Van Nostrand), has noted that "the prevalence of divorce, separation and illegitimacy among poor [city] Negroes should not come as a surprise" in view of the disrupting effects on family life of extreme poverty, poor housing conditions, the corrupting environment of the urban slum, and racial discrimination. "For when American society isolates the lower-class Negro from contact with

the general norms and prevents him from sharing in the rewards which follow from abiding by these norms, it guarantees the emergence of a ghetto subculture with different
standards of conduct, motivation and family life."

A major urban problem, then, is improving life in the
ghetto. The roots of the difficulties seem to be poverty, and
the way to eliminate poverty is through employment. If jobs
were available, Negro youths would stick to their schooling,
adult males would support their families, and the entire social
disintegration that results from poor family life would be improved. Providing jobs means an end to discrimination
against Negro workers in business, industry and labor unions. Training will also be necessary, a goal sought by the
Manpower Development and Training Act of 1962. The federal poverty program has also launched a Job Corps for
youths sixteen to twenty-one years old; the Neighborhood
Youth Corps, which puts teenagers to work in community-
betterment jobs; various programs to assist the poor in help-
ing the poor; adult education programs to attack illiteracy;
and small-business loans to increase commerce in the ghetto.

Negro leaders have urged much greater effort. Dr. Martin
Luther King, Bayard Rustin and others have called for a
massive "Point IV" program for the American poor similar to
the U. S. aid to underdeveloped countries. Dr. King has also
urged a 2-dollar-an-hour minimum wage for all workers and
a "massive public-works program."

Professor Daniel Moynihan, author of *The Negro Family,
A Case for National Action* (U. S. Government publica-
tion), has recommended direct action, such as increasing
mail deliveries to two a day and hiring indigent Negro men
as carriers.

The principle behind such actions would be to create gain-
ful employment for Negro men and youths. Once the Negro
male—and, for that matter, the unemployed male whatever
his race—is provided with productive work, his self-esteem
rises and his mental health improves. He is able to support

his family and assume his rightful and necessary role as head of the household. The self-defeating cycle of unemployment, poverty, idleness and female dominance of the family can be broken.

There will be probably not one program but many necessary to accomplish these goals. Some local governments have experimented with programs which employ welfare recipients on municipal highway, sanitation and recreation projects—and with good success.

Creating employment, rather than dispensing welfare funds, seems to everyone to be a much sounder approach to improving ghetto conditions. Welfare, or the "dole," has long been denounced by white and Negro leaders alike as a form of dehumanizing "colonialism" foreign to our American ideals of self-help and self-determination. But it seems unlikely that all welfare payments will disappear even with maximum employment. Many of the unemployed are unemployable. Illness and accidents create temporary unemployment. Widowed, divorced and deserted mothers of young children should not work. Government aid for such individuals and families seems necessary.

At the very least the existing welfare system should become an incentive to family stability and personal integrity. A suggestion has been made by urban leaders to dispense with the present welfare system and substitute a guaranteed annual income. The American people could afford, it is argued, an all-out attack on poverty by paying citizens the difference between the amount they earn and the sum established as a minimum subsistence income. The cost of this has been estimated at 20 billion dollars a year. Proponents of the scheme contend it would be cheaper than the present welfare system and the high cost of crime, health clinics and other social services for the poor.

Three consecutive summers of rioting lend urgency to all such programs. Shooting, burning and pillaging which can be quelled only by use of troops came as a shock to Americans believing ours is an enlightened, law-abiding nation. Continuation of such rioting perhaps qualifies as a national emergency.

Virtually every responsible observer had blamed the riots on the despair, impatience and frustration of ghetto residents too long denied the economic and social advantages of our society. These experts, too many to name here, consider that upgrading ghetto life is the only long-range solution to the rioting.

The summer riots are also seen as proof of the growing militancy of ghetto residents. Extremists using the slogan "Black Power" are openly advocating violence to force improvements in ghetto life. Moderate leaders, such as Dr. Martin Luther King, decry violence, both morally and pragmatically. They point out that Negroes are a 12-percent minority in this country, making insurrection (as some have called the riots) a fruitless endeavor. The militants reply that Negroes are an overwhelming majority in large areas of many cities and therefore can force change. Patience, they argue, has not worked. Impatience should now be expressed in a highly visible way.

Such militant attitudes are as old as revolution itself. Even the most cursory examination of history leads to the conclusion that the violence in the ghetto is predictable. Inequitable social and economic conditions lead to violence in England, France, Russia and many other countries, including our own. History shows, too, that alleviating the inequality, not temporary oppression, is the only solution to the violence.

Returning to the thought which began this chapter, it may be said that urban problems are not racial problems. There are problems of poverty and unemployment which spawn social and psychological difficulties, but these are problems of people. They happen to be a Negro problem because our central cities contain ghettos of Negro indigents. But there are also a lot of poor whites and destitute Indians. The conditions of Mexican Americans and Puerto Rican Americans and other ethnic groups vary only in degree from those of the Negro ghetto.

There is a race problem in this country: discrimination, the disreputable conception that somehow the color of a man's skin affects the sort of person he is. This discrimination certainly affects the urban problem of poverty for it makes it more difficult for the poor Negro to obtain employment and decent housing. But it seems undeniable that solutions to the problems discussed in this chapter would be easier if the attack were made on poverty and unemployment as economic and social evils, rather than as phenomena of Negroes.

☘ CHAPTER FIVE ☘

Organizing for Community Action

REHABILITATING THE POOR and despairing people who live in our cities is perhaps our most difficult and pressing problem, but it cannot be solved unless cities regain their spirit of community action.

All of our urban problems, including the overriding ones of power, money and planning, as well as the peripheral ones of poverty, housing, traffic and the others that have been mentioned, continue to exist only because urban residents allow them to. None of the problems will be solved by governmental action, although government must play a role. The key to resolving urban problems may well be community action.

Until very recently, urban residents wallowed in apathy—and many communities still do. Citizens sat out long traffic jams, accepting a five-mile-an-hour pace for a 100-mile-an-hour car. They breathed foul air, drank unsavory water, lived in tenements, looked upon vistas of unrelieved ugliness as if this was an inevitable state of affairs and impossible of change. They acted as though there just wasn't any other way to do these things.

When conditions became unbearable, those who could afford to moved to the suburbs, turned their backs on the blight and forgot it. Sure, urban problems existed, but they were the other fellow's. Let the politicians worry about it. Thus, our urban populace sank into apathy and were aroused only by a riot in Watts or Hough.

This public indifference to urban problems is itself one of the serious urban problems. As long as apathy exists, no real solutions are possible. The government can build a housing project, for example, but, unless the people who live in it take pride in it and organize themselves to maintain and improve it, the building quickly degenerates into a social tenement. The structure may be sound, but the quality of life remains less than stimulating. If residents are organized, involved and responsible, wonders can be worked.

One new development of the last decade is the trend toward community action. City after city is discovering how to marshal its citizens for action. The methods have varied from city to city, yet certain techniques have been used in common. To illustrate these, the community-action program in Baltimore will be described. Baltimore's problems were severe; therefore the accomplishments stand out the more. We will look first at Baltimore as it was, then as it is now, and finally we will examine the steps that were taken to effect the change.

Native author Gerald Johnson called it "the least known city in America." Its architects described it as "ugly and honky-tonk." To businessmen it was a "branch-office town" and the "factory district for Washington." To train riders it was the "tunnel between New York and Washington." To motorists it was an exasperation, and for a decade air travelers, even if they could find a flight there, landed at the "lonesomest airport in the world." A former mayor snickered, "Pittsburgh has Mellons, Baltimore has watermelons" and a Philadelphian lamented, "I have to go to Baltimore tomorrow. I'd better take a sleeping pill to keep up with the pace."

For years Baltimoreans were wounded by this disparagement, for unfortunately until quite recently there was more truth than humor to it. Baltimore was ugly, with great gray slums extending for mile after dreary mile along the city's main arteries. There were no expressways. A traveler going north and south along the East Coast had to beat his way through a snarl of vehicles and a maze of traffic lights along narrow, antique streets. Buildings were old, the citizens dowdy-looking, entertainment virtually nonexistent and the residents militantly conservative and pathetically dedicated to what they chose to call "inconspicuous consumption." Indeed, Baltimore, the nation's sixth largest city with almost one million people, was inconspicuous, a place to be avoided.

Progress was slow. The public auditorium was first suggested in 1902. Specific plans were drawn seven years later. The structure finally opened in 1962. An expressway running from downtown to the northern suburbs, first envisioned in 1904, was opened the same year—but only partially. Then there is the expressway linking the east and west sides of the city. In 1944 the city paid Robert Moses, former New York Commissioner of Parks, 50,000 dollars to select a route for it. The expressway still has not been built, nor has a route been agreed upon, even though 11 separate studies have been made. Baltimoreans are still arguing over it, a process known as the "Baltimore hassle."

The postwar problems of American cities seem a little worse in Baltimore, the traffic heavier, parking scarcer, buildings older. Crime was rampant. For a woman to walk unescorted on downtown streets after dark was unthinkable. Juvenile delinquency mounted. Narcotics addiction kept pace. Tuberculosis and venereal disease were scourges. For the upper- and middle-class citizens of Baltimore in the early 1950s, there was one way out—flight. The population of suburban Baltimore doubled to over a half million in a decade, creating disjointed, uninteresting suburbs ringing a sort of human Everglades. The loss of high-income citizens and businesses combined with greater demands for city services to create a pincer on the city's finances. In 1952, the city's reform organization, with the ponderous title of Commission on Governmental Efficiency and Economy, forecast municipal bankruptcy within a decade unless downtown property values improved.

One man described it in succinct terms:

> This town started to die with the Civil War, which destroyed most of its markets. But no one really noticed until after World War II. Then, all of a sudden, even the blind

could see this was a big, rag-tag city, choked by cars, strangled by age. Worse, nobody cared. Baltimoreans had lost their will to do anything about it. Besides, no one knew how to go about saving a dying city.

Yet today an incredible thing is happening in Baltimore. This inconspicuous city is being visited by formal delegations from such places as England, France, Germany, Sweden, Denmark, Australia, India and scores of emerging African and Asian nations. The Mayor of Miami and his staff inspected Baltimore, thus joining similar groups from Boston to San Francisco, Minneapolis to Fort Worth.

What they came to see is a city rebuilding itself. Square blocks in the heart of the city have been leveled and Baltimoreans are constructing a half dozen office structures, including headquarters for an insurance firm and the town's gas and electric utility. There is much more, not just on paper, but built or being built nearby, a 500-room Hilton hotel, a privately financed legitimate theater, three hospitals, two competing newspaper plants, a university campus, a medical school, several motels, including one with a revolving rooftop restaurant, underground garages for thousands of cars with old-world type public plazas atop them, that auditorium–convention hall and several high-rise apartment buildings.

The hub of activity is the corner of Charles and Lexington Streets. For decades this was the mercantile center of the city, one of the most valuable pieces of real estate in the world. Then, seemingly overnight, it was not. A department store which had flourished there for decades suddenly closed after the war and remained vacant. Its blank windows became an infuriating symbol of the deterioration of downtown Baltimore. Then, in 1961, bulldozers moved in and leveled the building. On the site was erected an office building, One Charles Center, and it in turn became the symbol of Baltimore's rebirth. It is only 23 stories tall, small as office buildings go, an onyx-faced structure designed by Mies van der

Rohe, in which the emerging skyline of Baltimore shines darkly.

With that building Baltimore began to turn the financial corner. Where the empty department store paid annual taxes of 62,500 dollars, the new building pays 275,000 dollars. The 23-acre redevelopment project of which it is part, Charles Center, will return the city 2.5 million dollars in real-estate taxes, compared to 531,000 dollars before rebuilding began. The sharp declines in downtown property values started upward early in 1964. Plummeting downtown retail sales figures bottomed out in January, 1963, and started a steady and sharp rise. Interestingly, the sale spurts are 2 to 5 times larger than those of downtown Washington, located only 40 miles away, which has had no central-city redevelopment.

The Miamians and Philadelphians come to see urban renewal working in Baltimore. Not just low-income public housing and high-income luxury apartments are being built, but middle-income dwellings as well. Work has been started on a 93-acre area in midtown which will include several hundred units aimed at persons earning 5,000 dollars to 7,750 dollars a year. Rents will range from 85 dollars to 129 dollars a month.

To further attract the middle class back downtown, an experimental group of townhouses is being built. One buyer is Walter Sondheim, Jr., former head of urban renewal. "I want to be downtown," he said. "I was born there. I never wanted to move to the suburbs. I only did because in-town living became intolerable."

Baltimore believes it was the first city in the country to find a way to rehabilitate older houses and save a declining neighborhood. By trial and error—often mostly error—Baltimore reestablished a decaying middle-class Negro neighborhood called Harlem Park by forcing owners to repair and modernize homes, building schools and playgrounds, and setting up functioning community organizations.

More important than the action is the belief that it is

unique. Baltimoreans speak of the new legitimate theater as the "first built with private capital in this country in 30 years." They have no proof of this, but they believe it—a radical change in attitude. As one man put it, "It used to be the only thing Baltimoreans had to brag about was that somewhere in the vast Greenmount Cemetery was the secret grave of John Wilkes Booth."

The new spirit is omnipresent. Baltimoreans sent salesmen for their port throughout the world and set up sales offices in London and Brussels. This activity together with a port-modernization drive enabled the city to maintain its third (sometimes second) ranking among U. S. ports in tonnage moved, despite the opening of the St. Lawrence Seaway, sharp improvements in competing South Atlantic ports and an increase in railroad freight rates.

Baltimoreans scrapped with the federal government for its share of jet traffic for that lonesome airport and won a unique adequacy-of-service case before the Civil Aeronautics Board. As a result, airlines were ordered to provide more flights to the city. Baltimoreans convinced the American League to make its first franchise change in 50 years and bring the Orioles there, then wooed teams in the National Football, National Basketball and American Hockey Leagues. Overnight Baltimore became host to circuses, ice shows and extravaganzas. Broadway road companies lengthened their formerly transitory stays and the Baltimore Symphony was invited to give a concert in Carnegie Hall.

Some expressways were built. A tunnel was thrust under Baltimore Harbor. Even downtown traffic was improved. In 1953 Baltimore hired Henry Barnes, now traffic commissioner in New York, gave him a virtually blank check and full power, and he moved the cars.

The confidence in the future strikes the visitor. "The trouble is we have never seen in America a truly beautiful, livable city," said developer James W. Rouse, who had much to do with rebuilding Baltimore. "If a new expressway is proposed, people know what to expect and can visualize it. But suggest a modern city filled with beauty, light, air and people who enjoy living there, and you get blank stares. We hope to show America such a city here."

Analysis of Baltimore's civic rebuilding process shows the prime movers are a group of 100 top businessmen called the Greater Baltimore Committee. It found a way to *involve* the most successful men in the city in civic problems and to apply to them the intelligence, resourcefulness and energy which made them successful men in the first place.

It was not easy. Efforts to form such an organization began in 1952 with a fund-raising drive. The Citizens Planning and Housing Association, a large, amorphous gathering of individuals and neighborhood-improvement groups, wanted to form a businessmen's committee to take an interest in civic affairs. To this end, a young woman went to see James Rouse, who operated a real-estate appraisal business with his brother, Willard, and partner, Hunter Moss. It was a shoestring operation, but they hoped to spread into shopping-center development, community planning and mortgage banking.

Rouse suggested several other businessmen for the young woman to visit and out of her efforts was organized a committee, named after Robert H. Levi, who was then executive vice-president of the Hecht Company, a department store. On the committee was Louis B. Kohn II, vice-president of Hochschild, Kohn & Company department store, a young man in his thirties, and Guy T. O. Hollyday, a former federal housing commissioner.

The committee, expanded by Willard Rouse, Hunter Moss and insurance executive Paul Swett, met irregularly and informally in the back room of a downtown restaurant trying to come up with a formula to interest businessmen in city problems. "After much discussion and investigating," Levi remembered, "we decided leadership could come only from a small group of men actively working on city problems. This way they would become involved in them and committed to their solution."

Ultimately the Levi committee envisioned an organization of 100 men, each representing one large company, who would pay sizeable sums of money to join. They would join as individuals, not as companies. Thus, they would have to attend in person. No assistant could substitute for them. "Our plan was to have a small paid staff," Rouse says, "so the members would have to work themselves." Finally, the group would work on one problem at a time, seeing it through to a solution. "We wanted a rifle, not a shotgun," says Kohn.

For almost two years Rouse, Levi, Kohn, Hollyday and the others labored to sell their ideas to Baltimore businessmen. Singly and in small groups they buttonholed the established leaders of the city, explaining, proselyting, reiterating the threat of municipal bankruptcy—and getting only glassy stares of incomprehension. Finally, when they were on the verge of giving up, decision was made to find one man, a member of the power structure, who was capable of enrolling the others. The choice was Clarence W. Miles, attorney, socialite, hard-driving, self-made millionaire. "He was a natural choice," said Rouse. "He had engineered the transfer of the St. Louis Browns to Baltimore, up till then the biggest coup ever performed in this town."

Rouse went to see Miles, made his appeal and hoped. Miles was enthusiastic. "I liked the plan at once," he says. "The town desperately needed an action group, not a debating society." With Miles committed, formation of the committee was easy. To say no to Miles was to deny a hurricane. He called on the same men Rouse and Levi had visited. Their stares were still vacant, but they could not refuse Miles. Thus, in January, 1955, the Greater Baltimore Committee was formed along the lines first envisioned in the back room. Miles, who had done in two months what the younger men had failed to do in two years, was elected chairman.

Miles and Rouse nurtured the fledgling organization like a new baby. As a first project, they chose a guaranteed success. As Rouse explained it, the City Council was considering a bill to build—at last—that expressway first considered in

1904. It was certain to pass, but Miles had the Committee support it and sent members to City Hall to testify. "That was important experience," Rouse says. "These men had never testified. Now they found it painless. Councilmen listened and, when the bill passed, our members felt they had been effective."

The Committee fought for the Maryland Port Authority, got involved in a prolonged "Baltimore hassle" over the site for the public auditorium and won when it was placed downtown, battled for air service, and worked out the urban-renewal system which is considered one of the best in the nation. That was again vital experience. A Greater Baltimore Committee subcommittee drafted the urban-renewal ordinance. They studied the problems, read books, interviewed experts. In short, these top-ranking heads of corporations applied to an urban problem their talents and energy. They didn't let the "other fellow" or "city hall" do the job.

During the first two years, Miles was essential. He drove toward action. Nothing could be tabled for "further study." Decisions had to be made and a stand taken. Equivocation was a sin and to do nothing was a disaster. Yet Miles kept the group on its rifleshot trajectory and out of politics and business squabbles. Very early one member tried to get the Committee to oppose erection of a competitor's factory. Miles denounced him. Later, a railroad executive confused his business interests with the city's need for air service. Miles criticized him in public and threatened to resign—and, as one member reported, "the public chastisement was temperate compared to his private comments."

Miles was succeeded by Charles H. Buck, who heads a title-guarantee company. He is known as "Mr. Integrity" in Baltimore and was able to break down initial political distrust of the Committee. An era of cooperation between businessmen and City Hall began. Committee members, as individuals, were appointed to a score of important state and municipal boards and commissions, as well as university and hospital boards. Thus the influence of the 100 spread throughout the city.

In the beginning, the Committee did little about the deterioration of downtown. The moving force behind this was another organization (also studded with Committee members), the Committee for Downtown, an association of merchants headed by J. Jefferson Miller, another department-store executive. The merchants wanted a master plan for rebuilding downtown and raised 150,000 dollars to finance it. The Greater Baltimore Committee put 75,000 dollars with it and created a subsidiary unit, the Planning Council, to prepare it. To take charge of planning the Greater Baltimore Committee chose Dr. David A. Wallace, now professor of architecture and city planning at the University of Pennsylvania.

Wallace and his topflight young staff began a series of interviews with downtown property owners and ran right into the apathy and disillusionment which had caused the Baltimore decline. As Dr. Wallace put it, "No one believed anything could be done and, so believing, nothing could."

"We decided," said Miller, "to try something we could do in a hurry, a smaller project that would give us experience for the bigger job and which would demonstrate what could be accomplished. You see, almost no one believed we'd ever get anywhere."

Out of doubt and disillusionment came Charles Center, a 23-acre, 125-million-dollar complex of office buildings, hotel, theater, stores, underground garages and plazas. Wallace's design, worked out in only five months, has been widely applauded for its feasibility and architectural excellence. *Architectural Forum* called it "concentrated, intricate, lively and full of changes . . . a celebration of city core qualities."

But when the plan was unveiled by Mayor Thomas D'Alesandro in March, 1958, the reaction of Baltimoreans, expressed over and over, was, "My grandchildren's grandchildren will not live to see it."

But the Greater Baltimore Committee had other ideas. It marshaled public opinion behind the plan. Newspaper publishers (again Committee members) gave great space to the project in news columns and on their television stations. Committee members spoke to hundreds of civic, service, religious and fraternal organizations. Every property owner and major tenant in the area was interviewed and his support enlisted. The Committee refused to allow the plan to be pigeonholed and pushed city officials to move it through legal channels. The Charles Center Management Office was created and Miller was persuaded to run it as a dollar-a-year man. Dennis Durden was hired to handle technical aspects of development. In order to lure him from his planning-consultant job, he was paid 26,000 dollars a year, making him the highest-paid public official in the state. The Committee also set up a special committee to help arrange financing for builders.

By 1960 the city was ready to accept proposals for the first building, an office tower to be erected where the department store had been. Three weeks before the deadline for submission of architectural designs, Durden and William Boucher III, the Greater Baltimore Committee executive director, pulled off a coup which made Charles Center a success.

"We all knew," says Boucher, "that the first building would set the tone for the rest. If it were good, the rest would be, too." Worried about the quality of proposals to be received, Boucher and Durden went to Chicago to solicit a bid from Metropolitan Structures, Inc., a firm which had made heavy investments in Chicago, Detroit and Newark. In three amazing weeks, Mies van der Rohe turned out a schematic design for the gem which now sparkles in Baltimore.

One of the disappointed bidders, wealthy Jacob Blaustein, erected a 30-story building across the street. After prolonged negotiations, the federal government agreed to erect an office building in Charles Center. Even longer, more delicate maneuverings were necessary before Miller and the Committee could land the Hilton hotel, theater and underground garages.

Progress was contagious. As one said, "The shock of seeing Charles Center going up, something no one ever believed would happen, has given the whole town a new lease on life." The Retail Merchants Association drafted plans for a mall over two blocks linking Charles Center with the main shopping district. The city planted trees along streets and even ousted court judges from hereditary parking places to create a small plaza. Plans to make over the naturally beautiful, but tragically blighted inner harbor area of downtown were prepared. Urban renewal projects were expanded. Private developers became eager to erect apartments and office buildings, downtown motels and stores. A promising regional planning council was established and an attack on metropolitan transit problems was launched.

The new spirit in the old city is everywhere. The city bought an automatic streetsweeper, a mechanical marvel of revolving brushes. But it failed in several neighborhoods because people wouldn't move their cars parked at the curb. Finally it was tried in Harlem Park, the rehabilitated Negro neighborhood. So strong was the community organization and so great the new-found pride, the sweeper went 80 blocks before encountering a parked car. Residents who formerly accepted litter as inevitable complained that the gadget was too wide to sweep the cluttered alleys.

Baltimore still has some staggering problems. Despite a great deal of effort to eradicate it, racial prejudice is a way of life. Crime is high and education is deficient in many respects. Tuberculosis is a scourge and other public-health problems keep pace. Politics is often more of a deterrent to public improvement than a goad. And, it is often pointed out, the activities of the Greater Baltimore Committee have kept the city from making its own Planning Commission an effective organization.

But it is the measure of community action in Baltimore

that the city's leaders believe these and the other problems can and will be solved.

The Baltimore method, which was itself an emulation of Pittsburgh's, has been copied successfully in a number of large and small cities. Other attempts at community action have failed. Out of the successes and failures have come some guidelines for community action against urban problems:

1. The business and professional leadership of the community must be organized into a relatively small group. All business rivalries must be put aside and the leadership must concentrate on city problems, one or two at a time.

2. The organization must be an *action* group, not a debating society. The members cannot delegate authority to others. They must work themselves and become personally involved in the problems.

3. They should tackle problems in the beginning which can be solved. Success breeds success.

4. The leadership must truly lead. It cannot develop plans and policies and seek to impose them on residents. The businessmen must become involved with the affected people in the community, explaining the nature of the plans and policies, why they are needed and why they will work. They must enlist the support of citizens and help them organize themselves to cope with their problems.

5. The community organization must work with government leaders, participating in governmental processes to see that proper actions are taken. This cooperation between private and municipal leadership is possible only if the private leadership remains politically nonpartisan.

None of this is easy, but cities all over the country are discovering ways to blend the public and the private, the powerful and the helpless into programs of community action.

CHAPTER SIX

Urban Renewal

THE PRINCIPAL TOOL which cities such as Baltimore have used to rebuild their community spirit as well as their bricks and mortar has been federal urban renewal.

A more imperfect tool is hard to imagine. It is such a slow-moving, exasperating, bureaucratic process that it sometimes defeats the purposes for which it was established. Urban renewal, particularly in its first decade of operation, produced more failure than success. Indeed, it often seemed the urban-renewal cure would kill the patient before age and blight did.

But in recent years, urban renewal has come of age. Federal and local officials have made some adjustments in the methods and, with experience, cities are learning to use it to constructive ends. Urban renewal, while still imperfect, ranks as a municipal godsend.

Urban renewal as a concept was formally proposed in 1941 and submitted to Congress in 1945. After prolonged and heated debate, the legislation was passed over bitter opposition in 1949. At this time the term "urban renewal" was not in use. Rather, the nomenclature was "urban redevelopment" and it meant "slum clearance," the tearing down of old structures and replacing them with new. The late Senator Robert A. Taft of Ohio, one of the principal drafters of the legislation, made it clear that he intended urban redevelopment to be restricted to slum housing.

The 1949 act established elaborate procedures for carrying out its objectives. In essence, the federal government would advance funds to local governments to finance the preparation of redevelopment plans. The city would declare an area to be a slum or redevelopment project, hire planners and architects to prepare plans for new housing, parks, playgrounds and other facilities. After this plan was approved by the federal government, the U. S. would advance funds to the city to buy the old properties—using its powers of eminent domain—and to demolish all the old structures. One of the conditions for plan approval was that residents be relocated in new homes. The federal government would pay part of these relocation costs.

After the land had been bought and the buildings razed, the city was to resell the land to private developers who would erect the housing and other structures called for in the master plan. The cleared land naturally sold at a lower price than the city had originally paid for it. The federal government agreed to pay two thirds of this "loss" or "cost" of urban redevelopment. Actually, the city did not have to put up the one third in cash. Its expenditures for schools, parks, highways and other public facilities in the project could be included in its one-third share.

In theory the plan offered distinct advantages. It would enable the city, and thus private developers, to assemble a large tract of land. Previously, private developers had been thwarted in renewal efforts because one or two property owners refused to sell. With the city's power of eminent domain at work, this difficulty would disappear. Then, too, good planning and urban design would be controlling. These advantages, plus the low cost to municipalities, generated widespread enthusiasm for the program among urban scholars.

The reality of urban redevelopment was somethat less rosy, however. Difficulties popped up which have plagued the program to this day.

For one thing it turned out to be an administrative nightmare. State and local laws had to be passed and municipal urban-renewal (or redevelopment) agencies established, all of which took time. And it seemed that all the procedural errors that could possibly be made in any new program, particularly one involving federal, state and local cooperation, were made.

The red tape of the program was a jungle. The city marked off a section as a project and declared it an urban-renewal area, a process often requiring city-council or even state approval. An application for federal aid was made to Washington, along with proper evidence of the need for such funds. Some weeks or months later the application was approved and planning funds were provided by Washington. Then the planning process was begun. Months, perhaps as long as two years would be devoted to this. Next, the plan went to Washington for approval. Washington officials went over the plan again, often duplicating the same work performed at the local level. The plan might be returned to the local level for redesign. Conferences and wrangling ensued. Many months elapsed before plan approval. More time disappeared before site purchase and demolition. These steps were just the major ones. There was a clutter of minor details, such as public hearings among project residents, advertising for and selecting bids. Various municipal boards and agencies had to approve plans. More wrangling resulted. From conception to completion, there were hundreds of steps in the renewal process.

The time from declaration of a project to site clearance was from two to five years. During this time all activity in the neighborhood stopped. Property owners did nothing to improve their properties. Why should they? The homes were to be torn down anyway. Tenants assumed the same attitude or moved out entirely, figuring they might as well get a head start on relocation. Often the simple designation of an urban-renewal area greatly accelerated its deterioration.

Site clearance had a devastating effect on areas adjacent to the project. The thousands of displaced families were supposed to be relocated into public housing projects, but there weren't enough of these. Nor was there enough standard housing. The displaced, fending for themselves, crowded into neighborhoods bordering the renewal area. These quickly deteriorated. For all the world it appeared urban renewal was ruining more neighborhoods than it was improving.

These difficulties just enumerated were the minor ones. The biggest problem with urban renewal as originally conceived was that private builders were not interested. The large, experienced builders were hard at work in the suburbs where there was a ready market for homes and where the problems were easier. They didn't have the procedural red tape to contend with. Tens of thousands of homes could be built in the suburbs before the first one was erected in the slums. With the nation's best builders uninterested, cities turned to inexperienced, even amateur developers who had to learn their business the hard way.

Another reason professional builders were uninterested was that the economics of urban renewal was all wrong. Even with the most advantageous federal mortgages, the builder would make far less money in downtown housing than in suburban—if he made any at all.

Thirty seconds with a paper and pencil and a builder could demonstrate the essential flaw in urban renewal as originally conceived. If housing were built in accordance with the approved urban-renewal plan, the poor people of the slums, who were supposed to move back into the redeveloped neighborhood, could not afford it. The lowest conceivable price at which modern housing could be built was about 60 dollars a room. A two-bedroom apartment would have to rent for 240 dollars a month, which exceeded the total income of many of the slum dwellers. If, on the other hand, housing was built which the original residents could afford, it was little better than that which had been torn down.

During its first five years, urban redevelopment, as it was still called, never got off the ground. Some 211 localities had expressed interest in the proffered federal money, but only 60 had reached the land-acquisition stage. Of the 500 million dollars which Congress had appropriated for uban redevelopment, only 74 million dollars had been "committed." In

One chaotic problem that cities have to face: traffic jams stretching out for miles at rush hour. (New York Daily News *photo*)

Commuters often must put up with similar traffic jams as they crowd into subway and other public-transportation systems. *(Photograph by Charles Harbutt, © 1966 Magnum Photos)*

Los Angeles, with its entangled metropolis, has solved some
traffic problems with multiple highways. *(California Department of Public Works photo)*

Construction is under way on the multimillion-dollar San Francisco Bay Area rapid-transit project, a 75-mile rail network that
should relieve the area's traffic congestion problems. *(Bay Area
Rapid Transit District photo)*

Slums, like this and worse, present a major social, economic and educational problem to cities. *(Photograph by Bruce Davidson, © 1967 Magnum Photos)*

Creating low-income housing, such as East Harlem Plaza in New York City, remains a most difficut task in urban renewal.

The Washington Square East project in Philadelphia, shown here in before and after photographs, is a prime example of the success of programs to rehabilitate existing buildings.

Just a few years ago, downtown Baltimore was ugly and economically unprosperous. *(Photo by Nat Lipsitz)*

One hundred business-
men organized to form
the Greater Baltimore
Committee to salvage the
deteriorating downtown
area. One Charles Cen-
ter, designed by Mies
van der Rohe, became
the symbol of Baltimore's
rebirth. *(Photo by Nat
Lipsitz)*

The 1,750-seat Morris Mechanic Theatre, part of Charles Center, was built entirely with private capital, encouraged by the
Greater Baltimore Committee. *(Photo by M. E. Warren)*

In Hartford, the Travelers Insurance Company agreed to finance the redevelopment of the blighted downtown area pictured above.

Constitution Plaza, a complex of office buildings and a hotel surrounded by a pedestrian walk, was the result.

federalese, "committed" means "put aside but not yet spent." Obviously, the program as constituted was not very useful.

Congress sought to breathe some life into the moribund program with the Housing Act of 1954. The administration of President Dwight D. Eisenhower urged Congress to think in terms of "renewal" of cities rather than redevelopment. Thus, the term "urban renewal" came into use. The 1954 Law made important amendments in the old one. The cities were to take a broader view than simply slum clearance. Efforts were to be made to halt the plunge of neighborhoods into blight by proper enforcement of zoning, housing, health, sanitation and other laws. School, hospital, playground, highway and other public projects were to be used to save neighborhoods. The totality of a city was to be kept in mind.

Of more specific importance, federal funds could be used to restore or rehabilitate (the popular expression) existing houses. This provision recognized that houses were wearing out faster than new ones could be built. Of immense importance was the provision that a portion—constantly made larger in the years that followed—of federal renewal money could be used in redevelopment and rehabilitation of *nonresidential* properties. With the Housing Act of 1954 and its further amendment in 1959, 1961, 1962 and 1964, urban renewal slowly began to work. By mid-1966, over 2,000 urban-renewal projects had been approved and over 5 billion dollars—3.4 billion dollars after 1961—had been committed.

Though urban renewal finally got off the ground, the ride was hardly smooth. Mistakes were frequent. Land was cleared only to lay idle for years, ugly scars of futility in cities. Impressive buildings were erected only to stand unoccupied. Waste and corruption were often the parasites of the program.

The critics of urban renewal, and they are legion, cite the mistakes as a basis for their argument that the system ought to be drastically altered or, preferably, abandoned altogether. But urban renewal, for all its faults, has had some startling successes. When success and failure are put in perspective, an evaluation of the worth of urban renewal becomes possible.

There have been alterations in the original urban-renewal process, but the basic system in use today is essentially that enacted in 1949. The federal government pays two thirds of the cost of planning, acquisition and clearance and participates actively in all these processes. Several efforts have been made to streamline the procedures, but they have had relatively little effect. Cities have had more practice in urban renewal and the elaborate processes are well-rehearsed, but urban renewal is still a procedural bog. Delay is the handmaiden of urban renewal.

This was pointed out by Milford A. Vieser, a Newark, N. J., business executive who has been active in renewal in that city. "It was only four weeks ago that Jack Parker—potentially our largest private developer—was able to break ground on a renewal plan for our city. It was five years ago, however, that he announced his plan for a vast multimillion-dollar renewal project in Newark." Mr. Vieser said Parker was ready to begin his Newark project within a year, but was delayed by the "endless stream of steps required between the announcement of a plan and the actual start of work on it."

Everyone agrees that the urban-renewal process ought to be streamlined, but no one knows quite how to do it.

One of the reasons for the delay in renewal is that it often turns into a political issue. One of the necessities of renewal is that the residents of the area agree to the change. Getting them to do this is often difficult. Local urban-renewal officials stage a series of meetings with neighborhood groups explaining the renewal process. This explanation is not very easy, considering the complex procedures. When the mistakes of renewal in the past are added to the normal opposition of individuals to change, a solid block of opposition quickly develops. In city after city, urban renewal has generated a storm of controversy.

There is no shortage of reasons for the opposition. One is simple greed. The property owners, particularly absentee slumlords, often derive profit from their dilapidated structures. They are unwilling either to lose the properties by acquisition and clearance or to invest in rehabilitation. Another reason is emotionalism. Urban renewal is seen as "socialism" or even "communism," with "big government" interfering with "free enterprise" and the rights of tenants and property owners to run their own affairs. This might also be restated as the right of people to live in squalor.

Some opposition inevitably attends the plan proposed by the city. Residents of a neighborhood do not like the changes proposed or they feel the essential character of the neighborhood will be altered or that proper facilities will be lacking. There are a dozen reasons for opposition to renewal projects, including the fact that residents object to the stigma of having their neighborhood declared a "slum." At best, the opposition delays the project and drains the energies of renewal officials into what is often political action. At worst, the opposition kills individual projects and sometimes urban renewal in its entirety. Frequently the issue ends up on the ballot. There is vigorous campaigning for and against it.

The most challenging task for urban renewal has been to provide low-income housing. The simple economics already mentioned, that new housing cannot be built at a price the poor can afford, remains a major problem to this day. Great effort has gone into finding ways to improve housing for the poor. For over 10 years the efforts, if anything, worsened the problem, but in recent years some new techniques have been tried which have brought some success. These will be reported in the next chapter.

The real success of urban renewal has been in erecting middle- and upper-income housing and, particularly, in rebuilding the downtown central cores of cities. Opponents of urban renewal read into such a statement not success, but failure. The major criticism of urban renewal is that the cities have purchased slums and sometimes perfectly acceptable neighborhoods, torn them down and erected an admittedly handsome collection of buildings. But these elegant new structures benefit the business community and upper-income groups. In short, the poor have been driven out to make way for the rich. Since the poor in the central cities are predominantly Negro, critics have dubbed urban renewal "Negro removal." With the lag in housing for the poor, the effect of urban renewal has been to worsen the condition of the ghetto.

Private developers may not be able to build housing for low-income groups, but there is great profit in building housing for upper-income groups and in erecting office buildings, stores, factories and other mercantile establishments. City officials want this type of structure. The buildings are architecturally attractive and create a better image for the city. Greater tax revenues stem from a single office building than several blocks of low-income housing.

Erecting projects of commercial enterprises and apartment towers has its own problems. Overbuilding has produced a glut of office space in some cities. Renting the new downtown apartments and townhouses has proved easier on paper than in reality. The buildings are lovely and the accommodations excellent, but the neighborhoods remain undesirable. The new buildings are often islands of beauty in a sea of blight. The view from the window is distressing. The children of the apartment dwellers have to attend public schools in the blighted neighborhoods. These factors make it difficult to rent new apartments.

Despite all of these valid criticisms, downtown urban renewal has been a huge success. The reason for this becomes clear when a metropolitan area is considered as a living organism. All living things have a core, a nucleus, a heart. When this dies, the organism dies. When the downtown core of a city dies, the result is not a city but a collection of incorporated suburbs each going its own way. There is no unifying force, nothing binding the various elements of a city together.

An American city is a melting pot. There are scores of nationalities, a variety economic strata, diversity in all things.

But if it is to remain a city, there must be a downtown to which all the diverse elements turn. What is downtown? The federal, state and municipal governments and courts, certainly. The headquarters of banks, insurance companies, stores, and principal business firms. All of the commercial enterprises have branches in the neighborhoods, but the unifying headquarters is downtown. The center of the city should house the principal cultural activities of the city, the library, symphony, opera company, legitimate theater. In downtown is the core of the recreation and entertainment, the best restaurants and nightclubs, parks, zoo, auditorium and arena. These and similar activities should be downtown if only to provide equal access from the suburban areas which encircle a city. A more cogent reason for keeping activities and institutions downtown is that it maintains the economic health of the city. The heart of the city has always produced the most tax revenues. It keeps the municipal government on a sound financial basis.

Prior to urban renewal, the downtown of most of our great cities (New York and Chicago were major exceptions) were in their death throes. The buildings were old and hardly any new construction was taking place. The hub was ringed with slums, choked by cars and festooned with vacant store fronts. The downtown tax base declined.

Downtown urban renewal has brought about a marked change. New government buildings have gone up. Business and industry have returned downtown to move into the new structures. Auditoriums and other facilities have made downtown a place to visit and enjoy, as well us to work and shop. The tax base has turned upward, improving city finances and making an attack on ghetto problems more feasible.

Immeasurably valuable has been the effect of the new downtown projects on the spirit of city dwellers. The effect of Charles Center on Baltimore has been described. In a score of other cities downtown renewal gave residents of the entire metropolitan area new pride in themselves and the beauty of the city and confidence that improvement was pos-sible. With improved spirit came all manner of activity unre-lated to the buildings being erected downtown. The streets were cleaner, houses neater. As people began coming back downtown for work and recreation, private investors leaped to provide them with new stores, restaurants, hotels. Change begat change and success bred success. And statisticians trotted out figures to show that every dollar of government money spent in urban renewal produced six dollars in private investment.

In the next chapter, we will examine in more detail the failures and triumphs of some of the major cities as they sought to rebuild their downtowns and eradicate slums.

CHAPTER SEVEN

Rebuilding Our Cities

PHILADELPHIA IS RECOGNIZED as the city which has made the best use of urban renewal. Profound changes have been and are being wrought in the historic "City of Brotherly Love" through the renewal process.

The 1965 annual report of the Philadelphia Redevelopment Authority showed 56 federally-aided renewal projects that were either completed or in progress and 21 other renewal projects that were financed by the city, private investors or nonprofit corporations or institutions. The federal projects had a net cost of 509 million dollars, of which 331 million dollars was to come from federal sources, 77 million dollars was to be invested in schools, parks and other municipal facilities; and 100 million dollars was to be provided by the city and state governments.

So much truly exciting development is going on in Philadelphia that this entire book would be inadequate to describe it. Only a few oustanding projects can be mentioned. The crowning achievement is Penn Center, now largely completed. In 1952, the Pennsylvania Railroad announced that it had—at last—decided to tear down the inner city's historic eyesore: the old Broad Street station and the mile-long stretch of elevated tracks that were popularly known as the "Chinese Wall." On the site was built Penn Center, a 120-million-dollar complex of transit and bus terminals, hotels, shops, restaurants, underground concourses, sunken gardens, pedestrian malls, apartment houses and modern office buildings. It provided a joy to the eye, a whole new and attractive image for downtown and ever-present proof that plans could become actualities.

The city's Food Center, an unsightly collection of whole-sale fish and produce markets adjoining Independence Hall, was moved to a new 100-million-dollar Food Distribution Center on what had been the town dump. If ever two birds were killed at once, this was it. The dump had been a smok-ing, unhealthy locale bordered by squatter shacks. The city collected a few thousand dollars a year in real-estate taxes. To prepare the food distribution center, the city invested 15 million dollars for land acquisition and improvements and private firms invested 85 million dollars in new warehouse and terminal facilities. The result of the effort is 2 million dol-lars in anual tax revenues for the city and potential jobs for 12,000 people.

With the food stalls which had blighted downtown Phila-delphia removed, the city began its Washington Square East project, which quickly recovered its Colonial name, "Society Hill," after the Society of Free Traders. Its landmarks are three towers fronting on the Delaware River. Designed by I. M. Pei, the towers have 720 apartments for middle-income families. Society Hill also includes a swimming pool and ap-propriate landscaping. A small shopping center is to be built adjacent to the towers. Over 700 historic old houses in the area are to be rehabilitated. Work is still in progress on these townhouses, but 5.3 million dollars has already been spent. Plans have gone forward for continuation of the Society Hill project westward. The Philadelphia Center of the Arts will be included.

North of Independence Hall a mall stretches for three blocks. It is being flanked by a new office building and federal structures, including the U. S. Mint, the Federal Office Building and Court House. In West Philadelphia, University City is in progress. Here five institutions, including the Uni-versity of Pennsylvania and Drexel Institute, are creating a comprehensive educational, scientific and research center. Studies are advanced for a major overhaul of Philadelphia's downtown shopping centers. The Market East project, eight blocks long from City Hall to Independence Mall, will consist of a huge terminal linking rail and wheel transportation. There will be ample parking and multilevel pedestrian concourses lined with shops. Aim is to lure shoppers downtown by providing parking as well as mass transit facilities, then permit them to walk in pleasant surroundings unimpeded by vehicles. The city has also made progress in low-income housing, which will be discussed later.

Urban renewal in Philadelphia has been a model of private and municipal cooperation. All the elements of successful city rebuilding can be seen.

An early start on urban renewal was an advantage. The Pennsylvania legislature adopted the Urban Redevelopment Law drafted by the Philadelphia City Planing Commission in 1945. This law, antedating federal legislation by four years, paved the way for the first redevelopment project in the nation, the East Popular Project.

In 1947, under the leadership of Edmund Norwood Bacon, soon to become City Planning Director, and architect Oscar Stonorov, an exhibit on urban design was held. Students from city schools participated, preparing plans, drawings and models for the Philadelphia of the future. Professional planners and architects joined with thousands of school children to stage the futuristic exhibition in a downtown department store. To the amazement of all, nearly 400,000 Philadelphians came to glimpse the city's potentials. These early plans still form the core of Philadelphia's programs. Even better—a point made over and over in Philadelphia—thousands of youngsters now grown to adults became participants in planning a greater city.

A year later, Harry Batten, head of an advertising agency, called together a small group of businessmen to discuss city problems. From this came the Greater Philadelphia Movement, an organization of top business and industrial leaders who apply their talents to urban problems. They are the thrust for community action, financing, prodding, guiding the city's progress as the Greater Baltimore Committee does to the south.

In 1949, the city gathered its ablest citizens on a Charter Commission to rethink and redesign the municipal government. This home-rule charter was accepted by the voters in 1951, at which time the first of a series of "reform" mayors, Joseph S. Clark, won office.

A key provision in the charter carried out by Mayor Clark was Philadelphia's greatly admired capital budgeting system. Each year the City Planning Commission prepares a six-year capital building program, that is, plans all the public expenditures to be made in the city for urban renewal, schools, recreation facilities, highways and much more. The first year of the budget becomes that year's actual capital budget when enacted into law by the City Council. In practice that body usually follows the recommendations of the Planning Commission. The results of this are orderly growth, sound fiscal policies and long-range planning throughout the city government. Top priority in the capital budget goes to urban renewal. Roughly 50 percent of the urban-renewal expenditures goes for residential projects, 23 percent to downtown projects, 18 percent to industrial projects, and 9 percent to university, hospital and other institutional needs.

By 1952, Philadelphia had forged the three cornerstones of its subsequent success: broad community participation and acceptance of planning, well-organized private leadership, and municipal government dedicated to orderly growth.

The key individual in the Philadelphia story has been Planning Director Bacon. A native Philadelphian, he has brought to the city a deep knowledge of modern urban design, coupled with a love of the city and its traditions. He has sought both to restore and to enhance the Philadelphia first laid out by William Penn. The historic landmarks, City Hall and Independence Hall, have become the focal points for downtown reconstruction. Colonial-style architecture, particularly in homes, has been preserved and new construction has sought to intensify the beauty and value of the old. Under Bacon's leadership an entire "school" of architecture has developed in Philadelphia which is now being copied around the country.

Philadelphia has also made use of the nonprofit corporation in rebuilding its city. Public-spirited citizens form a corporation to plan, finance, build and manage a project. The Greater Philadelphia Movement performed such a role for the Food Distribution Center. The Old Philadelphia Development Corporation concerned itself with the area around Independence Hall. The Philadelphia Industrial Development Corporation, formed in 1957 by the city and the Chamber of Commerce and supported equally by both, seeks to stem the flow of industry from the city. It buys, then sells or leases land and facilities to private industry and seeks to attract new factories to Philadelphia. Some other nonprofit corporations are Colonial Germantown, Inc., North Philadelphia Corporation, West Philadelphia Corporation, Philadelphia Diagnostic and Relocation Service Corporation and others. This use of nonprofit corporations is now being widely advocated. Congress is studying ways to foster their growth.

If Philadelphia benefited from an early start, interested government and broad participation, Boston is showing the rebuilding job can be accomplished even without these advantages.

If ever a city was dying it was Boston in 1960. Its central-city population had shrunk to under 700,000 while its suburbs—those 78 Balkanized municipalities—swelled to four times that size. The central business district lost 14,000 jobs in 10 years and the taxable assessments declined by 78 million dollars. The Port of Boston, so rich in history and commerce, was openly and accurately described as "dead." Big ships no longer called. Goods were trucked to Boston from the ports of New York and Baltimore. A new expressway effectively sealed off the port from the rest of the city.

Boston's troubles were manifold. Its median family income

was the lowest of the seven major metroplitan areas. At the same time, its property-tax rate was notorious, a staggering $101.20 for each $1,000 of assessed valuation—and properties were sometimes assessed at above their market value. In this tax climate, business left the city. Only two downtown department stores remained. The vacant store front decorated the city.

In the 1950s, Boston tried to reverse the downward trend, but only worsened it. The John Hancock Mutual Life Insurance Company erected the first postwar office tower. When it was finished, the assessment was upped from 6.5 million dollars to 24 million dollars, a tax load of 2 dollars per square foot of space per year. Since most commercial office space rents at 5 to 6 dollars per square foot, this tax load was prohibitive. Investors got the message: stay out of Boston.

There were grand schemes on paper. A plan was announced to replace old Scollay Square with a group of city, state and federal office buildings. The Prudential Insurance Company of America announced plans to erect an office tower, hotel and apartment houses in the Back Bay section. Both projects were still on paper in 1960. Urban-renewal processes were used to condemn and buy 38 city blocks containing 9,000 low-income residents on the West End. The residents were moved out and the area cleared for a cluster of high-rise, high-rent apartment houses, which have been described as "a banal grouping of blunt, balconied towers on a treeless plain." Adjacent to the area was the John F. Fitzgerald Expressway, an eight-lane incision that was the most costly highway ever built in the United States.

The year 1960 brought a new beginning for Boston with the election of John F. Collins as Mayor. He was only forty, a big and energetic man despite the fact that polio confined him to a wheelchair. He entered office without the usual political debts which had strangled most of the previous Boston mayors, and he set out to use his freedom to reinvigorate the city. His first step, and a key one, was to challenge the city's merchant leaders to help him. He put the city's problems on the line to a 16-man coordinating committee and challenged them to help him. The committee, which had supported Collins' opponent, began working with Collins to reorganize the city's tax-assessing office, building department and personnel policies. Thus, the city's power structure became involved in city affairs.

Next, Collins hired a man to head redevelopment, Edward J. Logue, a young, dynamic urban planner who had worked with Mayor Richard Lee in New Haven, Connecticut, to make that city one of the outstanding examples of urban renewal in the country. To lure Logue from New Haven, Mayor Collins paid him 30,000 dollars a year, more than either the Mayor of Boston or the Governor of Massachusetts earned. More important than money, Logue was given power. Officially, he was Development Administrator for the Boston Redevelopment Authority. But he also headed the Office of Development for the Mayor and thus was in charge of city planning. In most cities urban renewal and city planning are separate functions, prolonging the red tape and bureaucratic infighting. Logue held both jobs and eliminated confusion and delays.

Of all the urban-renewal administrators in the nation, Logue is considered a master of the mechanics of the process. He quickly went to Washington and persuaded the government to finance 10 simultaneous projects, saying, "We have got to have wholesale renewal. The trouble with this town in the past has been that there has been too much retailing—doing things for individuals, sometimes as political favors and sometimes just because that's the way they do things here."

Logue used his mastery of the renewal process to get Boston moving. He convinced the federal government to commit 105 million dollars to Boston, while spending only 72,500 dollars of the city's scarce tax money. Of the first 180 million dollars to be spent for urban renewal, the city's share will be only 7,850,000 dollars. Logue is accomplishing this by including the city's capital expenditures for schools, parks, highways and other improvements in urban renewal, thus reducing the city's one-third share of the cost. He used other federal regulations which enable the city to count in its share the investments hospitals, churches and universities have made in renewal areas. In the Scollay Square project, which Logue finally got going, the city invested no cash at all, making only site improvements, principally a 2,000-car parking garage which is to be leased to a private operator.

Government Center at Scollay Square, with its buildings designed by I. M. Pei, is the most notable progress in Boston, but much else has happened. Mayor Collins encouraged business investment by lowering the tax rate several years in a row and got the business community to invest in downtown. The Greater Boston Chamber of Commerce took over the task of replanning the waterfront and promoting its development to include marinas, an aquarium and new apartment houses. Designer Victor Gruen was employed to plan a new retailing district with parking for 6,000 cars and "pedestrian islands" where shoppers can move in comfort and safety. Great progress was made in improving low-income housing, both in building new low-rent garden apartments and in rehabilitating older housing. The 200-million-dollar Prudential project has finally been started.

Boston's progress has not been easy. There have been some horrendous mistakes and prolonged frustrations. Logue remains a figure of immense controversy. Almost every action he performs provokes criticism and frequently abuse. His efforts to establish urban renewal in the Charlestown section of the city provoked a near riot among residents opposed to it. All of the controversy surrounding Logue and urban renewal in Boston has made the task of rebuilding perhaps more difficult than in any other major city. But with each passing day the task gets a little easier.

St. Louis has used urban renewal and private redevelopment to achieve what residents believe is a miracle on the Mississippi. Like most American cities, St. Louis was a fortress of complacency, apathy and blight. No substantial building had been completed in the downtown area since 1927 and businesses were building their headquarters in the suburbs. Mill Creek Valley, a slum which included 5,000 outhouses, stretched just west of downtown, and the local skid row ran right past city hall. The symbol of St. Louis, which *Life* dubbed the "dowager city" in 1954, was the "most expensive vacant lot" in the world, at the intersection of 12th Boulevard and Washington Avenue. It was to have been the site of a grandiose headquarters building for the utilities empire of the late Samuel Insull. But when the Insull organization collapsed, the lot remained a hole in the ground. Efforts were made to buy it, but the Insull heirs, all British subjects, refused to sell. In 1946, a court authorized sale, and a year later an investor acquired it, but no improvement was made on it for 14 years. It was not until 1961 that a nine-story luxury motel was finally erected there. It was the first new room accommodation in St. Louis in 31 years.

The renaissance of St. Louis actually began in 1953 with the election of Raymond R. Tucker, a scholarly man, as mayor. He had an engineering degree and had been notably successful in the city's campaign against air pollution. Upon his election, he endeavored to widen his effect upon St. Louis, first by organizing its leadership and then by removing the legal roadblocks to progress. The former was accomplished by the founding of Civic Progress, Inc., a committee of business leaders in the mold described in other cities.

The first roadblock to progress was financial. Mayor Tucker began by winning a permanent earnings tax to increase revenues and take the burden off the property tax. Then, backed by Civic Progress, a 110-million-dollar bond issue was passed. Most of the money went for highways, which were sorely needed to link downtown with the suburbs. With money available, Mayor Tucker and Civic Progress tackled the city's archaic building code, which had long frustrated any attempts at modern construction. For exam-

ple, the code specified that any outside wall of a building
had to be of masonry construction, thus prohibiting the steel
or aluminum curtain wall which is used in most modern
office buildings. Seven years were needed to overcome technical and construction-union opposition, but a more modern
code was passed in 1961. Within weeks, plans for four new
downtown buildings were announced.

Another reform which opened the doors to progress was
the Missouri Redevelopment Corporation Law, which allowed the city to delegate its power of eminent domain to a
nonprofit corporation, much in the manner that was successful in Philadelphia.

As seems to be the case in every urban renaissance, a vis-
ual spark was needed to restore citizens' confidence in the
city and its progress. In St. Louis, the spark was a huge one.

In 1935, President Franklin D. Roosevelt had declared an
area along St. Louis' decaying waterfront to be an historic
site on which a monument would be raised in salute to America's westward expansion. The National Park Service opened
an office in St. Louis, but that was as far as the monument
got until after World War II. Then, in 1947, architect Eero
Saarinen won a nationwide competition with a design for a
monument in the form of a gigantic stainless-steel arch. Congress voted funds for the monument in 1956 and construction
started in 1963.

Each week as the gleaming structure rose, the pride of St.
Louis kept pace. When topped off in 1966, the arch stood 630
feet tall, the highest monument in the United States, 75 feet
higher than the Washington Monument in the nation's capital. Only the Eiffel Tower in Paris (1,056 feet with its television antenna) exceeds it. The arch, centerpiece of a planned
91-acre national park designated as the Jefferson National
Expansion Memorial, can be seen for 30 miles over the prai-
rie. Eventually elevators will be installed inside each leg to
carry visitors to the top. A museum, depicting westward expansion, will be erected under the arch. Already millions of
tourists visit the arch each year.

St. Louis had certainly discovered how to do things in a big way. Between 1958 and 1965 an estimated 355 million dollars was invested in downtown St. Louis. Among the major items is the new Busch Memorial Stadium, the 50,000-seat home of the St. Louis Cardinals. This is the heart of the Civic Center, which includes office buildings, a luxury motel and apartment buildings. Just beyond the "big wicket," as the arch is called, is the 52-million-dollar Mansion House Center, a cluster of apartment towers separated by three-story commercial buildings. St. Louis accepted the gift of the Spanish Pavilion at the 1964–65 New York World's Fair from the Government of Spain and raised 4 million dollars to move it to an area near the new stadium. It will be a memorial to St. Louis' Spanish origins. St. Louisians can dine on a river-boat moored at a levee. There are new stores, parking garages and buildings by the dozen.

Formal urban renewal got off to a slow start, as in many cities. The Mill Creek Valley slums was acquired and leveled —and remained leveled. "Hiroshima Flats" was the mocking term residents applied to the barren acreage. But now it is blooming. Its 454 acres will represent 200 million dollars in private investment in 1970 in apartment towers and offices.

San Francisco is another city often cited for its urban renewal. Under the leadership of M. Justin Herman, its urban-renewal director, San Francisco turned apparent disaster into progress. Foreboding stemmed from the discovery that the state was building the Embarcadero Freeway along the edge of town so as to block the city's spectacular view of the waterfront. The public outcry which resulted halted the expressway—it now goes nowhere in particular—and galvanized the city's leaders into more organized and enlightened planning.

Among the notable projects is the "Western Addition" just west of the downtown business area. A Negro slum, 11 by 4 blocks, is being replaced by apartment houses, office buildings, hospital, cathedral, trade center and other buildings.

The Golden Gate Project, profiting from Philadelphia's experience, is on the site of the old Central Market, which was moved to a better location. Three high-rise apartment houses have gone up with a cluster of blue-roofed townhouses in between.

Pittsburgh rightfully claims to offer the showcase of urban rebuilding. Its Gateway Center, at the confluence of the Allegheny and Monogahela Rivers, sparked private and public improvements in the Steel City valued in excess of 3.5 billion dollars. Completed in Gateway Center's 23 acres are seven office buildings containing more than 2 million square feet of rentable space; an 800-room Hilton hotel; a 27-story apartment house with 311 luxury units; four underground parking garages; four landscaped plazas where the Three Rivers Arts Festival is held annually; plus an assortment of restaurants and other facilities. About 140 million dollars was invested in the center, most by the Equitable Life Assurance Society of America. By mid-1965, assessed property values were 48 million dollars, compared to 9 million dollars in 1947. More than 20,000 people work there, five times the 1947 figure. For more reasons than the architecture, Gateway Center is truly Pittsburgh's Golden Triangle.

Gateway Center was only the beginning. There is the celebrated auditorium with the movable dome, a new stadium abuilding, Allegheny Center, a 78-acre, 50-million-dollar shopping and residential development only 12 minutes from the Golden Triangle, university campuses, hospitals and too much else to enumerate here.

The story of Pittsburgh's rebirth will be somewhat familiar to readers of this chapter. After World War II, Pittsburgh was a place to be avoided. Dense smogs were a daily occurrence, often so black street lights had to be turned on during the morning. Downtown, grass and trees were a rarity and not a single new structure had been erected in 15 years. Property assessments declined at the rate of 18 million dollars a year. The municipal government was 64 million dollars in debt and its borrowing capacity was down to 17 million dollars.

The prime ingredients that enabled Pittsburgh to rise from this slough were a dynamic mayor, the late David L. Lawrence; organization of the Allegheny Conference on Community Development, the original business group dedicated to community betterment. Its leader was banker and philanthropist, Richard K. Mellon. A 4-million-dollar gift from Mellon family foundations made possible Mellon Square Park in the center of the Golden Triangle.

Under Mayor Lawrence anti-smoke ordinances were enforced and strengthened. Then, in 1946, Mayor Lawrence announced plans for Gateway Center and created the Urban Redevelopment Authority to take charge of it. The Equitable Life Assurance Society was persuaded by financial and governmental leaders to develop the area and commit itself to an initial investment of 50 million dollars. Two railroads consented to remove rail and freight facilities. In 1950 nine of Pittsburgh's largest firms gathered in the City Council chambers to sign leases in advance of construction. Fifty percent of the office space in the initial buildings was rented before demolition had even started. By April, 1952, the first of three office skyscrapers was being occupied.

This brief résumé makes the process sound deceptively easy. On the contrary, long hours of work by city officials and members of the Allegheny Conference went into every step of the process. To persuade men and corporations to invest millions of dollars in what appeared to be a dying city, "hard figures" were prepared showing that the investments would be profitable. Investors needed to be assured that other investors would follow their lead. Unified public and private leadership accomplished these and many other tasks.

This brief coast-to-coast "tour" of city rebuilding concludes with Hartford, Connecticut, considered the most successful redevelopment of a central-city area. Constitution Plaza is a complex of five office buildings and a hotel surrounding a pedestrian terrace.

As in other cities, Constitution Plaza involved effort and leadership and struggle. The city bought the land and razed the buildings for the project, but had trouble interesting developers. Then the Travelers Insurance Company agreed to finance redevelopment, investing 35 million dollars. It became convinced that, even though it had its own building nearby, the tallest in the city, it had a stake in the remaining area. The flight to the suburbs by business firms had to be reversed, the company felt.

Hartford's Constitution Plaza has provided evidence anew that once a successful downtown project is started it ignites a rebirth of the whole downtown area. The Insurance City's biggest retailer, G. Fox, added a 12-million-dollar annex to its store, located across the street from Constitution Plaza, and Korvette's, another department store, occupied a long-vacant building nearby. The Phoenix Mutual Life Insurance Company, which had been planning to build in the suburbs, changed its mind and built the handsomest building in the city, a graceful, green-glass structure with curved sides that is connected to the plaza by a bridge. In Hartford, as in every city that has discovered the route to downtown rebirth, the energies and techniques that spawned that accomplishment are applied to other urban problems.

But if urban renewal combined with community action has been the means for rebuilding inner cities, it has not yet turned into the panacea for slums, the original intent of its Congressional proponents. But great effort and considerable ingenuity is being expended to make urban-renewal work in the ghetto. The ideal formula has not yet been discovered, but several promising techniques are being used.

The one technique that does not work is slum clearance. As has been pointed out, the ghetto dwellers are shoved into another area, which begins to deteriorate. One technique that works in certain situations is rehabilitation of existing housing. Dozens of cities are experimenting with this. With federal mortgaging it is possible to make house remodeling financially attractive to owners. The Urban Renewal Administration has reported some accomplishments in New Haven, Connecticut, which reveal just how attractive.

New Haven, long a leader in urban renewal, pioneered many of the techniques now being used in other cities. One of its projects, Wooster Square, was approved for execution in February, 1959, with a federal grant of 19 million dollars. When completed, the project will contain 4,600 people, who are predominantly Italian-Americans. Average income is between 4,500 dollars and 6,000 dollars. About 80 percent of the homes are owner-occupied. A typical home is a frame or brick Greek Revival house built 80 to 100 years ago for one family, but converted into two, three and four apartments. The most pressing needs were for improvements in heating, plumbing, electrical facilities and for extensive interior alterations to modernize ill-formed groups of rooms into modern apartments. The plans called for rehabilitation of 438 buildings. A study showed owners spent an average of from 5,500 dollars to 6,700 dollars on a structure housing two and a half to three families.

The Dwight area, approved for execution in September, 1963, with a federal grant of 7.7 million dollars, contained about 8,000 residents, of which 25 percent were elderly. The median income was slightly over 5,000 dollars and a majority of the homes were owner-occupied. Average rehabilitation cost per home was 3,900 dollars.

The Dixwell project, consisting of 256 acres, was approved for execution in October, 1960, with a federal grant of 12.7 million dollars. The population in 1960 was about 10,000 of which 73 percent was nonwhite. The median income was just under 3,100 dollars and a majority of the buildings with residential units were absentee-owned. Most structures were more than 50 years old.

Considerable progress has been made in all three areas,

with repairs and remodeling being performed both by absentee and nonabsentee owners. The neighborhoods have no radical "new look." The traditional architecture remains, but the homes are vastly more livable. And this was done without displacing the people who lived there.

Government financing made it possible. The Urban Renewal Administration provided specific examples of how it worked in Dixwell, the poorest of the neighborhoods. An owner-occupied, three-family house had a first and second mortgage plus attachments, for a total indebtedness of 15,076 dollars on which the owner made payments of $225.25 each month. Renovation of the third-floor apartment, including new windows and walls, new exterior siding on the dormers, new paint and reconstruction of the porch cost 2,485 dollars. Total indebtedness now exceeded 17,500 dollars, but new federal financing of the entire indebtedness reduced the monthly payments to $102.24 per month.

An owner-occupied, single-family house had an indebtedness of 2,400 dollars to which 6,500 dollars in improvements were added. Yet with new financing the monthly payment was reduced from $106.77 to $57.66. In an owner-occupied, six-family house, indebtedness increased from 12,278 dollars to 22,778 dollars, yet with refinancing the monthly payment decreased from $252.49 to $141.46. Another two-family home had its monthly payment cut from $126.34 per month to $75.79 despite a 2,500-dollar rehabilitation. An owner invested 6,270 dollars in improvements, but with refinancing his monthly payment was only $59.76, compared to 61 dollars previously.

Such attractive refinancing gives owners of blighted housing an incentive to rehabilitate their properties. Tenants can enjoy better housing without increased rents. The whole character of a neighborhood improves, particularly when the renewal agency invests modest sums in street improvements, playgrounds and schools. Such simple actions as planting trees and installing flower boxes change the atmosphere from despair to promise.

The process is agonizingly slow. Even after the owner has been persuaded to remodel, the actual work takes months sometimes.[1] The need is for a vast increase in the amount of mortgage money available. One solution is increased federal appropriation, but most planners and redevelopment officials believe much of the capital must come from private sources. The nonprofit redevelopment corporation appears to offer great promise in this area. The corporation, backed by funds from banks, insurance companies and other lending institutions, as well as public funds, arranges refinancing at low interest rates in low-income areas.

There is a trend among major U. S. industrial corporations to invest in housing rehabilitation on a nonprofit or low-profit basis. Foremost in the trend are those firms which make building products, who will profit from the increased use of their goods and services. But firms unrelated to construction are beginning to finance rehabilitation. In great pride Philadelphia recently unveiled the first home rehabilitated in a section of North Philadelphia. Forty percent of the cost of the construction loans was supplied by Smith, Kline & French Laboratories, a pharmaceutical house. The firm's main headquarters is in the neighborhood and company officials were concerned about the deterioration of the surrounding housing. Planning Director Bacon called the project "the greatest thing that ever happened." Mrs. Jose Martinez, who moved into a new three-bedroom apartment with her husband and children, said, "I've been watching them fix it. I've dreamed about it every night." Her ten-year-old daughter added, "I'll have a room of my own." Mr. Martinez said, "It's going to be a nice neighborhood when they fix it up." The Martinez family had lived across the street, paying 18 dollars a week for four rooms. The new, larger apartments rent for 63 dollars a month.

[1] Experiments have been tried to speed rehabilitation. In one, the contractor enters through the roof and, with a crane, lowers entire prefabricated rooms into place. Proponents claim an entire house can be remodeled in 48 hours and tests have supported this.

Rehabilitation of the type described so far has its limitations. It appears to work best in stable neighborhoods where residents can be organized into committees and associations to participate in the planning. The groups work with renewal officials to delineate the problems and to develop solutions. From this action comes community pride which continues the improvements long after carpenters and painters have departed.

One of the finest examples of this was Harlem Park in Baltimore, a stable, but rapidly deteriorating Negro neighborhood. Renewal plans called for a new school in the area. Then the cluttered, useless interiors of each block were to be cleared. Residents were given their choice of either a grassy park or a blacktop playground in the interior courts. At the same time extensive remodeling of homes was to occur. In the beginning the project experienced great difficulty. Lending institutions were reluctant to refinance mortgages. More serious was the bungling of community relations by the renewal agency. Residents often misunderstood what was being attempted. There were personality clashes between renewal workers and community leaders. At one time the project seemed a certain failure. But the renewal agency revised its community relations, sending in new personnel and, more importantly, changing its attitude. Instead of imposing rehabilitation from city hall, the agency began to work with community associations to meet goals desired by them. The project then went ahead and today is one of America's showplaces of rehabilitation.

The deep ghetto where poverty is most grinding offers more challenging problems. The housing is too dilapidated to be rehabilitated and the residents too poor to afford anything but the worst housing. Neighborhoods are so unstable as to preclude effective community organization. Even if a "fix-up" campaign is carried out, deterioration quickly sets in again.

In such areas rehabilitation of people seems as vital as rehabilitation of housing. The whole lexicon of activities which were discussed previously needs to be considered—education, training, jobs, health, sanitation, public transportation. But better housing must be offered, too.

One promising technique being used is subsidized housing. A builder erects housing for low-income families, which he rents at a loss at prices the poor can afford. The government or a nonprofit corporation makes up the loss and guarantees the builder a predetermined profit of 6 percent. Thus, an apartment which has a break-even rent of 75 dollars a month might be rented for 50 dollars. Public funds would be used to pay the landlord the other 25 dollars a month, plus a small profit. This technique, which will work in rehabilitation as well as new housing, has engendered widespread enthusiasm.

Solving the problem of urban housing appears to require a broad-approach with many techniques in use. The erection of high-rise middle- and upper-income apartments will be helpful, if it attracts suburbanites back into the city and opens the suburbs for middle-class Negroes. Slum clearance and erection of low-income public housing will always play a role, particularly if the housing is subsidized. Rehabilitation, using both public and private funds, offers the greatest promise if increased far beyond present practice. In some projects, notably in Philadelphia, both new public housing and rehabilitation are being blended in the same neighborhood.

To be most effective the housing rehabilitation must coincide with efforts toward human rehabilitation. There must be increased economic opportunity and a wide range of facilities to make neighborhoods fulfill their promise as centers of the good life.

CHAPTER EIGHT

Urban Education

WITH ALL THE successful effort to improve the quality and quantity of American education since World War II, it would seem unlikely that education would still rank as a major urban problem. But it does.

Education will always be a "problem" in the United States, for we set perhaps unrealistic national goals for ourselves. We accept education as the first task of government. We aim to provide maximum education for every individual, which we interpret to mean that every individual has the right to receive, at public expense, the education and training which will enable him to make full use of his talents, not just his intellectual capacity, but his mechanical, scientific and artistic abilities. More, we view education as a preparation for life and expect public education to prepare young people for citizenship, homemaking, parenthood. In performing these tasks, we expect education to improve the homelife of students, enhance the quality of neighborhoods, diminish racial tensions, alleviate other social and cultural problems, and cope with the special educational needs of the lame, blind, deaf and mentally retarded.

The task is hopelessly utopian and our "problems" nearly all relate to our unrealistic goals. If we were more pragmatic about education, we could take more pride in our accomplishments. Enrollment has greatly increased since World War II. The flight to the suburbs required a vast increase in the size of formerly bucolic school systems. At the same time that the number of children being educated increased, the quality of education markedly improved. More professionalism for teachers was obtained. Standards were raised and salaries increased. The curriculum was improved, with greater emphasis on scientific, mathematical and technical subjects. A variety of special educational programs was initiated.

Despite all that has been done, we still have educational problems because of our high goals.

The problem of educational quantity has changed. There was a time in the 1950s and early 1960s when simply providing a classroom and a desk for all the children who needed them was a paramount difficulty. But the immense building program of the last two decades has considerably lessened the problem. There are still areas with classroom shortages. High-school facilities, the most expensive to build, are especially inadequate, but it is our colleges that are most underequipped. The postwar baby boom created first a need for elementary classrooms, then junior and senior high and, at this writing, college facilities. Because the birth rate has started to decline and, somehow, erecting buildings is relatively easy, the classroom shortage is no longer a major problem. This is not to say it is not *a* problem. It simply is a less compelling one.

If anything, our difficulty with facilities is that we do not make use of what we have. One of the less comprehensible aspects of education is our waste of school buildings. We erect structures costing several million dollars apiece, then use them not more than one third of the time. Pupils attend, at most, eight hours a day for 180 days a year. There are some summer classes, adult-education sessions, meetings and athletic events in school buildings during evening hours, but the sum of all usage cannot possibly exceed one third. The Russians, in contrast, reportedly run three classes a day in the same schoolrooms.

There is no intent here to get into the relative merits of the two-shift and 12-month school programs, except to say that many responsible individuals have urged them. Our present underuse of facilities persists because parents object to the inconvenience of a change. Sending children to school in shifts or operating buildings 12 months a year would mean that parents would have to rearrange their work, leisure and vacation schedules. Working mothers would be inconvenienced if their children were not in school till evening. The fixture of the summer vacation would be eliminated in a 12-month system.

The biggest problem of educational quantity is the shortage of teachers. At the start of the 1966–67 school year, the Research Bureau of the National Education Association estimated there was a national shortage of 141,800 elementary teachers and 27,500 high-school teachers. The elementary-level shortage was termed "critical." There were shortages of teachers for high-school English, mathematics, natural and physical sciences, commerce, home economics, library science, industrial arts and other subjects. Many other subject areas had an adequate supply of teachers, particularly social studies, physical education, music, art and speech. No one expects this situation to be remedied for several years.

Why is there a shortage of teachers? There are just about as many reasons as there are people to propose them. A major one, certainly, is the population squeeze. The postwar baby boom is being taught today by prewar and wartime populations. Relatively few of the babies born after World War II have reached teaching age; thus the demand for teachers exceeds the population supply. In a few years a greater balance should develop.

Another factor in the shortage is the federal legislation which set up new educational programs for underprivileged children. These will be described later, but at this point it should be mentioned that finding the teachers to staff these programs has been difficult.

What is often termed a "high" turnover among teachers is a factor in the shortage. Recent figures showed that 11.4 percent of all teachers resign or retire annually for various reasons. It is difficult to judge whether this figure is high. Many industries have much higher turnover rates. Yet, a teacher goes to a great deal of specific effort to become a professional. Perhaps it is reasonable to expect fewer of them to leave their chosen field.

The causes of teacher dissatisfaction have been widely discussed. Teaching is a demanding occupation, requiring physical stamina, patience, creativity and organizational ability. The demands of the job and simple fatigue can compel a person to quit. Many have criticized unrealistic standards for teachers. They not only need to fulfill requirements in college, but often must take special courses in local history and other subjects and pass a special examination in addition to the regular state test.

A major cause for teacher disatisfaction is alleged to be inadequate salaries. Particularly in the 1950s and early 1960s, teacher organizations lobbied vigorously for higher salaries. These efforts were successful in bringing beginning salaries in most metropolitan areas to the 6,000-dollar to 9,000-dollar range. Peak salaries range between 9,000 dollars and 14,000 dollars. In their laudable drive for higher salaries, spokesmen for teacher groups tended to speak only of the figure on the paycheck, neglecting often to place a monetary value on the considerable "fringe" benefits that accrue to a teacher. These include tenure, which guarantees a high degree of job security, generous retirement, sick leave, regular vacations, and a 190-day work year compared to 240 in most occupations. Then, too, there are excellent promotional opportunities to principal, supervisor and superintendent, some of whom earn over 20,000 dollars a year. While further salary improvement will continue to be a goal, the injustice done to teachers in the past seems to have been largely corrected. The increased number of men and women entering teaching bears this out.

What can be done about the teacher shortage? Change in the population patterns will help a great deal. Emphasizing the appeal of teaching, both occupationally and compensatorily, can attract people into the profession. The campaign for higher salaries has left an unfortunate residue of public opinion because the negative aspects of the profession were emphasized for so long.

The quality rather than the quantity of education poses the greater urban problem. In particular, urban education fails to meet the needs of the child from the ghetto, especially the Negro child. Rectifying this situation is the great challenge to education today.

The roots of the problem were expressed by James E. Allen, Jr., Commissioner of Education for the State of New York. Addressing senior public-education officials from seven large states, he said most state departments were "poorly equipped" to meet the educational needs of big-city slum areas because the departments had been set up to help rural children.

The rural focus of education permeates our school systems. Consider the problem of a Negro first-grader. His is a tenement world. His entire life has been spent in a cold-water walkup flat in a blighted neighborhood. He plays on the front stoop or the street corner. Fun is a game of stickball in the alley. In school, however, he learns to read from books which depict a white boy and girl who live in a charming white house with lawn and trees and flowers. They have a dog which is their inseparable companion. For adventure, they visit a farm or firehouse, a quaint church down the street, a kindly old man who tells them stories. They have both a mother and a father. The mother stays home and the father goes off to work in a suit and a white shirt and carries a briefcase.

The world described in this ghetto child's reader might as well be on the moon, so foreign is it to his existence. If he can imagine it at all, he can hardly identify with it. The effect of such readers is to imply the inferiority of his existence and thus his own inferiority. If he gives up on the whole educational process at the beginning, who is to fail to understand it?

Great effort is being expended to prepare primary readers which relate to the world of the ghetto child. In those which have been published so far, at least some of the children depicted are Negro. The characters live in the city and their world includes apartments, sidewalks, traffic, parks, playground, stickball and the other realities of city life. The child can identify with the characters and take pride in his existence and gain insights into how he might live more satisfactorily in the city.

The rural focus of education is present in many subtle ways, for education assumes that the student likes schools, wants an education, has understanding parents, pleasant living conditions and a place to study. As we know, the reverse is true for a significant minority of city children. Their curriculum ought to include information about how to kill rats, the importance of obtaining an education, how to study in an overcrowded flat, the operations of welfare agencies, the role of the policeman, where to get a bath, proper sanitation procedures and much, much more. While learning reading, civics, science and other subjects, information about the exigencies of ghetto life should be imparted to the slum child.

Great effort is being made to report correctly the history of the American Negro. Both white and Negro children can benefit from knowing the heritage and accomplishments of Negroes, rather than portraying the United States as a white man's country with a subservient Negro class. A case in point is the gross historical error that the "carpetbag" state legislatures in the South following the Civil War were corrupt and inept. On the contrary, some of these Negro-dominated legislatures passed very progressive legislation.

The problem of educating the ghetto child—or, as the educators prefer to express it, the "disadvantaged child"—requires far more than some new readers and textbooks. This youngster is intellectually and culturally deprived. For example, when he enters the first grade, he has a much smaller vocabulary than his middle-class fellows. Studies have shown that the average "undisadvantaged child" has an oral vocabulary of 10,000 words, with some having twice that. The slum child may have a vocabulary of 2,500 words.

This occurs because ignorance breeds ignorance. His parents, if present at all, are not educated. Their conversation, which the child hears, is severely limited to the affairs of the ghetto, getting enough to eat, paying the rent, stretching the welfare check. Parental discussion of public policies, international affairs, and cultural matters is severely limited. Indeed, one of the severest handicaps of the ghetto child's entering school is that he is unfamiliar with "proper English." His may be a dialect composed of a different accent, strange slang, unique expressions. Teaching this child to read the "proper English" which he hasn't heard becomes difficult.

The cultural deprivation of the ghetto child keeps pace with his language deficit. In most cases he hasn't been read to, learning about animals and foreign lands and strange places he has never seen. He has never seen mountains, the seashore, a forest, a majestic river. His culture has denied him a visit to a farm, a tour of an art gallery, a concert, a picnic or a shopping expedition with his mother through a glittering department store. How can the word "cow" have meaning to him when he has never seen one? To be sure, he has television, but slum children, like all young children, watch cartoons, horse operas and improbable comedies.

Some writers have seen the improvement of ghetto culture as a task of education. This is more accurately the task of society, but education certainly plays a prominent role. The disadvantaged child desperately needs advantages. He needs exposure to a world beyond his cramped horizons to learn of the greater culture of which he is a part and in which he must live.

A massive campaign to ameliorate the ghetto child's educational deficit has been launched under federal auspices. The arm of Operation Head Start and other programs is to enlarge the culture of the preschool child. He is enrolled in kindergarten, where he can be exposed to books, movies and conversation he has never heard before. He is taken on trips, sent to camp and exposed to art, science, and much else previously denied him. At the same time, social workers contact his parents to endeavor to improve his home life and parental attitudes.

Education is only on the frontier of this long-neglected, immensely complex problem. Great difficulties are to be surmounted. One type of difficulty was spotlighted during the Conference on Pre-School Education for the Disadvantaged Child, sponsored by the National Education Association and the Magazine Publishers Association. During a question-answer period these comments were made from the floor:

> I was interested to watch an experiment on Long Island where upper-middle-class white men raised a lot of money, bought a property and established a child day-care center. They planned for 80 children. By beating the bushes, they were able to get seven. We're planning some magnificent things here in our ivory tower, but how are you going to get your foot in the door of that slum lady in our district who has five or six kids hanging on her skirts? I had to go back four times to even get the door open. Now, I can make all these wonderful plans and pour a lot of money down a rathole, but what are the reactions of the people here today? How are we going to communicate with these people and get them in the program?

The question was answered by Mrs. Catherine Brunner, coordinator of school-admissions project in Baltimore. She said the problem was first to find the children who needed help and then to "sell" the mother "or whatever adult is responsible for the child" on the program and "why it's really worthwhile to have the child involved." Then, Mrs. Brunner added:

> It isn't easy. It takes a lot of legwork. It takes a lot of time and effort to build communication with the people and the neighborhood. But once you can sell the idea and its benefits to some of these people, they, in turn, can assist you in going

out in the community to talk to others. I don't think there is any easy way to do it.

As these comments indicate, there is a backlog of distrust and ignorance to be overcome if Head Start or any other program to assist the disadvantaged child is to be successful. At this writing, it is difficult to measure the effectiveness of these programs. Many are still experimental. There is great need for far larger appropriations, more teachers, better training, systematized techniques. But there have been some undeniable successes, and educators are optimistic that these programs can be effective when applied on a mass basis.

But the preschooler is not the only problem. The teenage dropout is a tragedy, too. The U. S. Office of Education reports that every third child in the fifth grade fails to finish high school. Since this is a statistical average for the country, the figures for the ghetto are much higher, over 70 percent in some urban neighborhoods.

The dropout pays a high price for his lack of education. Unemployment or, at best, menial employment, poverty, ignorance, prejudice, cultural deprivation are his "gains" from failure to finish school. A generation ago the dropout could find employment on the farm or the assembly line. Today the farm population has shrunk and the assembly line is being automated out of existence. There is a labor shortage in many areas, but the skills in demand are technological, mechanical, electronic and scientific. The dropout, unless he returns to some form of schooling, has the rewards of the technological age denied to him.

The culture of the ghetto creates great pressure for a young person to become a dropout. Culturally deprived before he ever entered school and taught with improper materials and by less than desirable methods, he lags behind his middle-class companions. He reads poorly and thereby learns less, so that, when his IQ is tested, his scores are lower and he appears "dumb." Worse, he has little motivation to overcome his obstacles. What good will his hard-won education do him? Racial discrimination denies him the white man's job and the white man's labor union. His parents and friends put little value on education, so why should he? If he is going to be sentenced to the ghetto all his life, he might as well get an early start on getting used to it.

Changing this pattern is a complex task, involving a better start in school, remedial-reading programs, motivational efforts. But encouraging the dropout is as much a social problem as an educational one, for conditions in the ghetto must be improved. Better housing, increased employment for men —in a word, *hope*—must be brought to the slums if youth are to appreciate the value of an education and persist in obtaining it. The dropout, like the disadvantaged child, is a subject of intensive study by educators. Great effort is being made. Many experimental programs are being launched. Success has encouraged optimism.

This résumé of some of the principal problems of urban education must include the thorny thicket of school desegregation. Briefly stated, the problem is this: although school segregation was held unconstitutional by the Supreme Court in 1954, the deeply ingrained neighborhood-school policy has enforced a high level of segregation.

Particularly in the elementary grades, the school building has traditionally served the youngsters living in the neighborhood. The building is a hub of the neighborhood, a meeting place for community groups. Local pride and desire for a good school enhances the quality of education offered. The neighborhood-school policy has played a vital role in the success of public education in this country by enabling the community to become involved in education.

But when housing patterns are segregated, the neighborhood school appears to widen the separation between the races. Negro children go to one school and white children to another and the dream of the 1954 decision that the two races could learn to live in harmony and mutual understanding is denied. Schools may be legally desegregated, but in fact schools remain segregated, especially in cities.

Civil-rights leaders of both races have long realized that one way to break down housing patterns and enforce greater mingling of the races would be to discard or alter the neighborhood-school policy. One means, tried in many communities, is to transport white students from one neighborhood to a Negro school in another and vice versa. The effect of this is to abandon the neighborhood policy along with its virtues. A second approach is to redistrict the neighborhood schools to achieve more equitable racial balance. Thus, a predominantly white and a mainly Negro district might be changed so that the two schools were more equally white and Negro.

For the last decade white parents have objected vigorously to all such proposals. They cite all the advantages of neighborhood schools. They point to the disruptive influence that busing children and placing them in other schools would have. They contend the children brought in cause overcrowding or lower academic standards for the Caucasian school. Or, they insist the white school will not meet the peculiar needs of Negro children. But in whatever clothing the reasoning is attired, the result is racial discrimination. Particularly in the North, desegregated housing remains the hardcore point of discrimination. Whites will work with a Negro, eat with him, socialize with him, but living next to him is another matter. This attitude is breaking down rapidly, but it remains the core of the de facto school segregation issue. Quality of education is a consideration in the debate, to be sure. It is argued that both whites and Negroes will benefit from school integration—and if the races don't learn to live together as children, when will they? But the main issue in school desegregation is housing. If a school is desegregated, then its neighborhood becomes desegregated.

De facto school segregation has caused a storm of controversy. Demonstrations, protests, parades, stormy meetings have resulted from nearly every effort to bus children or redistrict schools.

The controversy has placed school administrators squarely in the middle. They cannot please everyone. If they do what is wisest and morally appropriate, they are denounced by either the proponents of civil rights or of neighborhood schools. The school superintendent is wrong if he does and wrong if he doesn't. And, in our democracy, school executives cannot ignore the wishes of the community. They must adjust their actions to public opinion.

The segregation problem has made the big-city school superintendent's job the most thankless in government. No better example exists than Dr. Benjamin C. Willis, General Superintendent of Schools in Chicago. He took over the system when it was in a low state and built it into one of the finest in the country. During the 1950s and early 1960s, when there was a severe classroom shortage, he built schools so rapidly and economically that Chicago was able to eliminate half-day sessions. He raised salaries, convinced the state legislature to approve bond issues, got ever larger appropriations for schools. At the same time that he was demonstrating talent for solving the financial, tax, construction and recruiting problems that beset the superintendent, he was showing himself to be a significant educational innovator, launching major curriculum changes and instigating new programs which greatly improved the quality of public education in the Windy City.

Yet in the end he fell into disgrace over de facto school segregation. Adhering to the neighborhood-school policy, he built schools where they were needed, unmindful of the color of the children's skin. Civil-rights leaders interpreted his actions as racially motivated and accused him of attempting to enforce segregation by building schools inside the ghetto, rather than on the fringes where racial balance could occur. Demonstrations occurred. Dr. Willis was denounced as a racist and harried by protest marchers both at his office and at his home. He was made into a symbol of white man's prejudice. Negro groups were rallied to demonstrate against him. In the end, he was driven from his post—and the schools of Chicago remained largely segregated.

The solution to the school-desegregation issue must lie in

the hearts of men. It is also true that the hearts of men can be changed by exposure. Any mingling, particularly by children, tends to break down the misunderstanding and hostility that have plagued both races. Therefore busing and redistricting cannot help but expose the races to each other and change attitudes. But surely it is unfair to saddle education, which has enough problems of its own, with what is essentially a housing issue.

Until white attitudes change, only minimal progress toward school desegregation seems possible. The goal of equal opportunity for Negroes will be a long time coming. Dr. Willis said during an interview that he felt his task as an educator was to provide all people, regardless of skin color, with the best possible education and opportunity to earn a living. He felt that, if Negro children got that opportunity, they would find employment and relief from poverty and thus break out of the ghetto.

Others, notably Negro civil-rights leaders, believe education must play a key role in exposing the races to each other and breaking down segregated housing patterns. The conflict between these views is far from settled, nor does a solution appear in sight.

❦ CHAPTER NINE ❦

Crime and Criminals

IN JULY, 1965, the President of the United States appointed a National Crime Commission of 19 members to seek new ways to combat the growing menace of crime in this country. Leading judges, attorneys, professors, police officials and prosecutors were named to the body.

In announcing the Commission President Lyndon B. Johnson said:

> The present wave of violence and the staggering property losses inflicted upon the nation by crime must be arrested. . . . I hope 1965 will be regarded as the year when this country began in earnest a thorough, intelligent and effective war against crime. The time has long since arrived for this nation to discard obsolete and unworkable methods of detecting and apprehending criminals.
>
> We must come to grips with the problems of punishment versus rehabilitation, of protecting society from criminals while at the same time working to prevent the development of potential criminals. The commission obviously cannot solve all the problems related to crime. I do ask it to commit wisdom, energy and experience to the simple need of this and any civilized society: the safety of its citizens.

The Commission's report, issued 18 months later, suggested "sweeping and costly changes in criminal administration" throughout the nation and recommended more than 200 changes it believed should be made. These ranged from generalities involving policy to specific crime-fighting measures. To what extent these recommendations are adopted by local, state and federal governments remains to be seen, but at the very least the Commission left no doubt there is a major crime problem in the United States.

Indeed there is. In 1965, the Federal Bureau of Investigation reported that Americans committed 2,780,000 serious crimes, 6 percent more than the previous year. Fourteen out of every 1,000 inhabitants were victims of a serious crime—and that figure reflected a 35-percent increase since 1960. What crimes? There were 5,600 murders; 34,700 aggravated assaults; 68,400 armed robberies; 118,900 unarmed robberies; 1,173,000 burglaries; 2,500,000 larcenies: and 486,000 auto thefts. Total property loss exceeded 1 billion dollars.

FBI Director J. Edgar Hoover reported that crimes of violence increased 35 percent in five years, crime against property 47 percent. In fact, crime in this land of liberty increased 6 times faster than the population between 1960 and 1965. Every hour someone was murdered, two women forcibly raped and a dozen stores robbed. Every minute a car was stolen and two businesses burglarized. Not only was there more crime, but the criminals were getting away with it. Fewer than 2 out of every 5 robberies, 1 out of 4 burglaries, 1 out of 5 larcenies were ever solved. These facts led Richmond, Virginia, attorney Lewis F. Powell, Jr., to remark when he was president of the American Bar Association, "There are valid reasons for criminals to think that crime does pay and that slow and fumbling justice can be evaded."

By all means. The take from organized gambling in the United States is estimated at between 7 and 10 billion dollars a year. These illegal profits are increasingly being invested in legitimate businesses with a thoroughly corrupting influence. Hoodlums and racketeers have moved into such fields as real estate, construction, labor unions, vending machines, laundries, taverns and restaurants, bottling plants, trucking firms, wholesale meat and produce, and even firms listed on the major stock exchanges. All of this can be documented—and it is a document of fear and shame.

Only one more fact will be listed. All the figures given so far were for 1965 as compared with those of 1960. The FBI reports for the first nine months of 1966 showed crime had increased 10 percent, double the 1965 rate.[1] Thus we have an immense and rapidly worsening problem.

Few matters in our times have so disturbed and preoccupied our leaders as crime. Great effort and study have gone into finding solutions. An almost inconceivable outpouring of words and opinion has resulted, the most observable effect of which has been self-defeating controversy.

An attempt will be made in this chapter to avoid adding to the controversy by examining the problem with some perspective and objectivity. We can begin this effort by pointing out that crime is an urban problem only because so much of our population lives in cities. Suburban crime is growing faster than urban crime, and rural crime is on a par with urban crime. In fact, the large increase in crime is a world-wide phenomenon.

Three factors dominate both the causes and the solutions of the crime problem. They are society, the law and the police themselves. Much of the controversy has occurred because individuals have sought to cite one factor as *the* cause. Only when all three are given equal importance can some of the controversy disappear.

Crimes are committed by people, and our society both causes and encourages people to lawlessness. There are many crime-inducing factors, some of which will be covered briefly.

Crime is nourished in the ghetto. The conditions which have been described previously not only encourage crime but make it a way of life. Grinding poverty, the idleness of unemployment and despair, all found in abundance in the ghetto, make it difficult to see the advantages of a law-abiding life. A man will steal to feed his family, to get some kicks out of life, to win stature as a brave and enterprising individual, even to go to prison, for a life behind bars is an improve-

[1] And the Presidential Crime Commission reported that a survey of 10,000 citizens indicated that a majority of the crimes actually committed are never reported to the police for various reasons!

ment on the existence of some in our society. The jail at least offers shelter, food, warmth, clothing and security. Many a habitual criminal has found a home in prison.

The ghetto breeds crime because the whole pattern of life seems to penalize the lawful and favor the lawless. The honest citizen has a most difficult time finding a job, while the person less discriminating about legalities can enjoy an income. Participating in the numbers racket, making book on the races or tabling a few bets on athletic contests provides a lot of "employment." Or, if the fellow has the stature and disposition, he can find "work" using his muscles to shake down store proprietors, "settle" with persons who have "welched" on gambling debts or failed to pay loan sharks. He can make a few dollars by driving a private car as a taxi in contravention of city taxi laws. He can push a little dope or peddle pep pills, participate in the welfare-check fraud, pick a purse or two, shoplift a few items, tap a till by rifling the cash drawer while the proprietor is distracted. For a woman there is prostitution.

This brief list includes by no means all the ways a person can earn an illegal dollar. Almost none of it is in the category of serious crime. The risks of capture and punishment are relatively slight—certainly less than the risks in trying to live honestly. None of this should be construed to mean that all poor people are crooks. All that is being said is that in the ghetto there is opportunity, a rationale, and a climate which encourage lawlessness. And when a person succeeds at minor crime, it induces him to try more serious and daring crimes.

No explanation should be needed concerning why nondeliberate crimes of violence occur in the ghetto. Crowded living, despair, and ignorance certainly present opportunity for anger and uncontrolled emotion. Murder, rape, and assault somehow occur more easily when a person has less to live for.

Ghetto life seems to breed disrespect for the law. A man can easily see the law as his enemy. It protects the person who has money and property, but offers less protection to the man who has neither. The law, meaning the policeman, puts no food on his table or roof over his head. Instead, the policeman tells him to move along when he congregates with friends on the street corner. The law, in the sense of regulation, makes it difficult for him to earn a living and surrounds him with rules governing his conduct and even his personal life. When a rich man breaks the law, he can hire lawyers and accountants to hide the fact or represent him in court. The poor man is more at the mercy of the law.

Disrespect for the law in the Negro ghetto is fostered, too, by the racial issue. The law is the white man's law, enforced by white men. Until very recently, the law kept Negroes from voting, sitting in a public restaurant, sleeping in a hotel, buying a home in certain locations. The policeman who enforced the law was a white man, often arrogant and occasionally physically brutal to the Negro. Certainly the white policeman was not nearly so zealous in protecting the Negro citizens as the white ones "uptown." The Negro went before a white judge and a white jury and learned that he got a stiffer penalty and shorter justice than his fair-skinned fellow citizens. Much has changed, but until recent years the law was an instrument of Negro oppression.

The Negro has learned, too, the simple lesson that breaking the law was one way to improve his lot. Thousands of sit-in, lie-in, chain-in demonstrations were the tools that got the discriminatory laws changed. Protests caused the police to change their attitudes and methods. Rioting, burning and pillaging brought quick results wherever they occurred. The Watts section of Los Angeles received more attention and corrective action within a few weeks after the riot than in the previous decade. The lesson has not been lost on young Negroes. It resounds in the slogan "black power," which urges not necessarily violence but the use of concentrated Negro economic, social, cultural, and political power to change the law and society.

All of these factors combine to cause high crime rates in the ghetto. The solution, easy to talk about but difficult to

effect, is to improve the conditions in the ghetto. Simply en-
larging the police force and cracking down on lawlessness
will not materially affect the crime rate and may, in fact,
worsen it. Nor do court procedures affect the causes of crime.
"Changes in court procedure," said David Acheson, former
United States Attorney in Washington, D. C., "would have
about the same effect on the crime rate as an aspirin would
have on a tumor of the brain." The social conditions which
cause crime in the ghetto must be alleviated.

Crime is hardly a phenomenon of the poor. The sharp increases in suburban crime indicate this. But again, we iterate
that our society encourages lawlessness. This shows in our
ambivalence toward crime. We consider ourselves a law-
abiding nation, yet we have admiration for the crook as long
as he is not sadistically violent. Robin Hood, Billy the Kid,
Jesse James, John Dillinger and others—criminals all—are
part of our folklore and have an attractive aura about them.
Our national image of the criminal is a handsome, dashing,
devil-may-care fellow enjoying his ill-gotten gains amid wine
and wild, wild women. Some of our greatest rewards go to
the worst criminals. At this very moment, the heads of our
national crime syndicates live privileged existences on vast
suburban estates, with country-club memberships and direc-
torships in corporations. Their sons go to exclusive colleges
and their daughters have society debuts. One New York
hoodlum took justifiable pride in the fact that his son was
appointed to West Point. The corrupt politician is elected
year after year and nearly everyone takes pride in his ability
to fix a ticket. A little cheating on the income tax, some influence at city hall, an acquaintance in the rackets, a bet or two
on a football game, smuggling items through customs, etc.,
are not so reprehensible as admirable and "justifiable" acts.

Added to this confusion in attitudes toward crime and
criminals are changed moral attitudes. A generation ago it
was easy to discriminate right from wrong. Our parents and
grandparents lived by a more rigid set of rules about rela-

tions with their fellowman. A person might not always abide by the rules, but he was sure that he ought to. Marriage, for example, was forever and the only framework for sex. This may still be the dominant opinion, but a significant segment of the population, rightly or wrongly, believes that divorce is to be recommended and that sex has a role other than in marriage. Taking a human life used to be a cardinal sin other than in time of war. Now there are those on the fringes of society who suggest mercy killings for deformed babies and the chronically ill may have some merit.

Our moral confusion has been abetted by psychiatry. Many hold the view that what a person does is less important than his reason for doing it. We explore a man's origins, his relations with his parents, his social conditions, his mental state before judging the guilt or innocence of his acts. It may be argued that such attitudes are more humane (or pure foolishness), but this book need not judge. All that matters is that our more tolerant views toward morality and ethics and human conduct create a climate in which we prejudge the law and rationalize the breaking of it. The rationale can range from a conviction that the law is wrong to a belief that a little excitement is good for the soul, but the crime rate goes up in both instances.

We live in a time when seemingly all of our attitudes, institutions, and traditions are being questioned. As a nation, perhaps as human beings, we are questing for greater truth and better methods. It is a dynamic and challenging time in which to live. But one of its by-products, found both in the deepest ghetto and in the most fashionable suburb, is an increase in crime. As difficult as eradicating the ghetto will be, altering the attitudes which permissiveness, license, doubt and irresponsibility have induced will be the harder task. Eventually, perhaps not in this century, the moral confusion will be resolved (temporarily) and society will again embrace a specific set of rules. It will be possible to alter laws to conform to the attitudes then in vogue. Until that millennium arrives and we can tell right from wrong with more certainty, we may well have a continuing crime problem.

The law itself is the second factor in crime. Part of the problem has already been intimated: many criminal laws are archaic, inconsistent, unjust and just plain wrong. They fail to reflect the changed attitudes of sizeable segments of society, and it is axiomatic that no law can be enforced in a democracy which the people do not want enforced. Our criminal codes are cluttered with old laws no policeman would think of enforcing, if indeed he could. But this clutter is unfortunate because both the policeman and the citizen are required to decide for themselves which laws ought to be enforced—and that is the essence of anarchy, not government.

There are deeper problems with the law which were expressed during an interview by Chief Judge Edward M. Lumbard of the United States Court of Appeals for the Second District, in New York.

> There has been no substantial change in criminal law for 300 years. Criminal law has always been the stepchild of the legal profession, full of abuses which have been shoved under the rug. We have left the criminal law to the least competent, least trustworthy elements of the legal profession. We are long overdue in revising and updating criminal procedures.

Judge Lumbard is chairman of a committee of the American Bar Association which has been studying and recommending changes in criminal law and court procedures. Among the matters under study are rules for interrogating suspects and other prearraignment police practices, press coverage, pretrial deals between the prosecution and the defense for a guilty plea to a lesser charge, equitability of sentences (different judges impose different sentences for the same crime), and the pardon and parole systems. For the first time in history, the best legal minds in the country are probing the defects in our criminal procedures. Only good can result.

The spur for the reevaluation of criminal law is a series of

United States Supreme Court decisions.[2] In more than a score of major decisions the high court has sought to humanize criminal law and broaden the rights of defendants. The effect of the decisions has been to upset long-established police and criminal-court procedures. Some of the principal changes forced by the court were:

Defendants in a trial have a right to know in advance the evidence the prosecution will use against them.

Evidence obtained by an illegal search and seizure (an example would occur if police seized evidence without a proper search warrant) cannot be used against a defendant at his trial.

The Constitutional right of a person not to testify against himself has been broadened to include unwitting testimony taken by secret wiretaps and recording devices.

Testimony given before one investigative body (such as a legislative committee) cannot be used in a subsequent criminal trial.

Every defendant has a right to be represented by a lawyer at his trial, either at his own or at government expense.

When a suspect is arrested, the police cannot refuse him the right to confer with his attorney.

The police must tell a suspect of his rights not to confess or give a statement and that everything he says may be used against him. If he asks to see an attorney, all interrogation must stop.

A suspect must be promptly charged with a crime and taken before a judge for arraignment and the setting of bail.

This series of Supreme Court opinions has had two principal effects—it is not an exaggeration, perhaps, to call them *cataclysmic*—on law enforcement. The first was procedural. The high court did not issue the decisions at one time. Instead, they came over a decade, beginning in the mid-1950s. In deciding the legal issues in one case, the Court left some

[2] For a fuller discussion, see the author's *Tides of Justice* (New York: Delacorte Press, 1966).

questions unanswered until the next case. In the meantime, lower courts, prosecutors and the police would be uncertain whether their actions were legal. This uncertainty hindered law enforcement and aided criminals.

An illustration of this began in June, 1964, when the Court ruled in *Escobedo v. Illinois* that, if a defendant was refused the right to see his lawyer who was waiting at the police station, his subsequent confession could not be used against him at his trial. One of the many questions that stemmed from this ruling was whether a man's confession could be used if police failed to tell him of his right to call a lawyer. This question was raised in many criminal cases. California courts said the confession could not be used, while Illinois courts said they could. Both decisions were appealed to the Supreme Court, which refused to hear either case and thus left both rulings stand.

The confusion snowballed. The U. S. Court of Appeals for the Third District, which sits in Philadelphia, ruled such confessions were unacceptable as evidence, thus freeing two men convicted of murder. The Court of Appeals for the Second District, which sits in New York, ruled such confessions could be used in evidence. With neighboring appellate courts reaching opposite opinions, Chief Justice Joseph Weintraub of New Jersey directed the courts of his state to ignore the supposedly binding federal rulings and abide by state laws.

Eventually, the Supreme Court did consider this issue and decided that confessions could not be used if police failed to tell a suspect of his rights. But almost two years had passed, a time of confusion and semiparalysis in law enforcement. The police and prosecutors were afraid to act because they might be acting illegally. Unfortunately, this slow-motion alteration of criminal procedures is still going on and will continue into the foreseeable future.

The second serious effect the Supreme Court decisions had upon law enforcement was that old police methods were discarded without any suitable substitute. An example of this is to be found again in confessions. The police have long solved crimes by arresting suspects, interrogating them, obtaining confessions and then charging them with a crime. Now, this procedure has been made so difficult as to be unusable. Detectives can still take a confession, but only after they have informed the suspect of his rights to remain silent and to call a lawyer, who assuredly will tell him not to confess.

Police officials to a man insist that such procedures grossly hamper their efforts. They say that most crimes do not produce physical evidence, such as fingerprints, bloodstains, threads and fibers which modern crime laboratories can transform into evidence. Only the perpetrator of a crime, police insist, can reveal what occurred and, sometimes, even that a crime happened. The police have a duty, not only to solve crime, but also to prevent it by arresting hardened criminals and unbalanced individuals who prey on society. In violent crimes, such as murder, rape, assault and armed robbery, the police have to act quickly to arrest criminals if society is to be protected. They cannot wait for the slow process of finding physical evidence. Interrogating the suspect and persuading him to confess, police insist, is the quickest way to accomplish this goal.

Critics of police practices insist that the confession is not that necessary, that detectives use it in lieu of a search for admissible evidence. A huge controversy rages over which of these arguments is correct.

The important point here is that the police, stripped of interrogation as an investigative technique, have been hard-pressed to find a substitute. Many departments have stopped all questioning of suspects. The New York Police Department is establishing a special interrogation room wherein impartial observers will be on duty full time and sealed cameras and recording devices will operate around the clock so that a full visible and oral record of the interrogation will be available.

It would seem that in time the police will come up with new and probably improved investigative techniques, but in

the meantime there can be little doubt that law enforcement
has suffered at a time of rising crime rates. The police nearly
everywhere feel discouraged and frustrated in their ability to
combat the crime menace. They cannot question suspects,
seize stolen goods even when the suspect carries it on his
person, obtain a search warrant unless they have much evidence beforehand. They cannot use wire-tapping and listen-
ing devices to obtain evidence except in unusual cases. As
detectives have said in interviews, "We are just about down
to solving those cases in which the fellow comes in, surren-
ders and insists upon confessing."

There is great controversy whether the current paralysis of
law enforcement is caused by the policeman's failure to develop new techniques or by the fact the courts' efforts to protect defendants have left the public unprotected. It may well
be both. In time a greater balance between criminal offense
and police defense will be reached, but meanwhile the
achievement of that balance is an urban problem.

The third leg of the crime problem is the police themselves. There are legions of fine, dedicated officers and some
police departments do strikingly good work under adverse
conditions, but there is mounting evidence that police departments in general are suffering from hardening of their
administrative arteries because of poor personnel, archaic
methods and insufficient funds.

Police inefficiency is difficult to write about in a short
space. There are tens of thousands of police departments and
each one may be progressive in one aspect and anachronistic
in another. In order to illustrate what can be wrong with a
police department, recent revelations concerning the Baltimore Police Department will be cited. At the request of
Maryland state officials, the International Association of
Chiefs of Police (IACP) sent to Baltimore a team of investigators. Their 600-page report was a textbook on just about
everything that could possibly be wrong with a police department. John E. Ingersoll, director of the IACP Field Operations Division which prepared the report, said, "In the

more than 110 police agencies we have surveyed, we found none with as many problems as Baltimore. . . . It must be said Baltimoreans have never known good policing."

The IACP discovered that Baltimore taxpayers supported their police admirably. Of the 10 largest cities in the nation, Baltimore ranked third in per capita expenditures for police, second in the number of policemen per 1,000 inhabitants, and fourth in officers per square mile. Yet so mismanaged was this force that, when the IACP experts deployed the men where they were needed, Baltimore had 136 officers left over with nothing to do. Surfeited with policemen on whom a 27-million-dollar annual budget was lavished, Baltimore was nevertheless saddled with a crime rate that was twice the national average and an automobile-accident rate twice that of Cleveland and three times that of Houston.

The IACP found the department was organized for futility. The commissioner and chief inspector had dual, confused and often overlapping authority. Worse, these two men didn't speak to each other except in public or under duress.

Beneath these two were a clutch of inspectors with crazy-quilt commands. One inspector was in charge of two geographical police districts—*and* rackets and narcotics investigations *and* the riot squad. Another district inspector supervised the hunt for runaway husbands, dispensed uniforms and checked on sanitary conditions in restaurants. The commander of detectives was also in charge of building construction and maintenance because the chief inspector, who had formerly held the job, "liked to work with my hands."

Worse even than this structure were the organizational omissions. The department had no intelligence section to combat organzied crime, no internal inspection to determine whether orders were being carried out, no planning and research to consider ways to improve the department. Said Mr. Ingersoll, "The department functioned as it had in the 1920s, resisting all change. Those methods aren't good enough today."

The force had serious personnel shortcomings. At a time

when most industry was demanding a college education or at least advanced technical training from employees, the Baltimore Police Department reduced educational qualifications to eighth grade *or equivalent.* Thus, the IACP found that 60 percent of the men had never finished high school and of its 3,700 members only 21 had college degrees.

Considering these educational levels, the wages paid policemen were not too bad. Patrolmen earned from 5,000 dollars to nearly 6,500 dollars a year, but the department had arranged that some older men were paid less than newer men and officers were paid less than the men they commanded. A new sergeant received 450 dollars a year less than a senior patrolman, a senior sergeant 820 dollars more than a new lieutenant and so on through inspector. All of these men were regularly "touched" for contributions to the "fender fund" to pay for minor damages to police vehicles.

The promotion system was the most implausible ever designed by man. The method was based on a written examination, performance ratings and seniority in such a way that hundreds of men could qualify for promotions. The commissioner was not required to promote top men on the list. In 1963, with 122 men eligible, the commissioner made sergeants out of the 40th, 47th, 55th, 70th and 106th men on the list, the last achieving a test score that was only one third of a point from failing. At another time the commissioner gave stripes to the 117th man on the list, who was only 84/1000th of a point away from ineligibility. But perhaps the worst example was the selection of a captain who ranked 47th on a list of 48 eligibles. This topsy-turvy system of rewarding incompetence was enacted into law by the State Legislature in 1961 at the enthusiastic urging of ranking police officers.

After men of limited education and doubtful competency were promoted, they received absolutely no training for supervision. A patrolman was declared a sergeant and allowed to sink or swim. An investigator attached to the state's attorney was put in charge of the large, high-crime Western District without an iota of training and virtually no experience in the day-to-day operations of a police district.

There was no plan for career development. Captain Wade Poole spent 23 of his 25 years in the Western District, where he learned to deal effectively with race problems and neighborhood street crime, then was put in charge of the Central District, where he had to cope with vice, rackets and professional criminals. Another man spent his entire career in the traffic division, then was suddenly declared commissioner. Instead of being moved around for orderly training and experience, instead of refresher training and courses in public administration, policemen were expected to spend years being "good cops," before being precipitously made supervisors and administrators.

The inevitable result was gross mismanagement. Purchases were made from favorite suppliers, rather than by competitive bidding. After purchasing was turned over to the city, the prices for police cars dropped 10 percent. Not only were the cars overpriced, they were the wrong kind. Accident investigators were outfitted with special white station wagons in which they carried equipment that would fill a small shopping bag. The department spent 100,000 dollars a year maintaining two emergency or rescue vehicles on the streets at all times. Analysis revealed the vehicles answered only one call every 24 hours and only 1 percent of those calls required any of the expensive equipment hauled around in the truck—equipment largely duplicated by the fire department. While lavishing equipment where it was not needed, the department "saved" money by using inadequate 6-cylinder radio cars instead of more powerful 8's, and so deprived detectives of vehicles they had to double and triple up just to get around town.

The IACP found mismanagement throughout the department. Men worked around the clock coding information into computers which turned out a stream of largely useless and entirely unread summaries and reports. Until mid-1965, budget preparation was at best hit and miss, and there was no formal filing system in use.

If the leaders of the department were not too adroit at public administration, it would have been expected they would at least have been effective in police supervision. The IACP was perhaps most devastating in its criticism of the deployment of men. The survey report ticked off item after item: the department operated a "Hotel, Pickpocket and Very Important Persons Squad" consisting of one captain, two lieutenants and three sergeants to direct the work of six patrolmen in the solution of an average one crime daily and one VIP escort per month. The department maintained 15 horses at great expense, yet there were few crowds to control so the mounted police wrote traffic citations at the rate of two or three a day.

So riddled was the department with jealousy that patrolmen investigated crimes, rather than turn them over to detectives, leaving detectives to patrol streets for muggers and purse snatchers. Result? Early in 1965, patrolmen labeled four violent deaths as accidents. Days later, after clues were gone, pathologists discovered the deaths were stabbings and shootings. The IACP found the department topheavy with officers—one out of every five men was a sergeant—most of whom did the work of patrolmen and did not supervise. Traffic policemen directed traffic at corners where there was no traffic—just because a patrolman had always been at the corner.

Perhaps the most damaging indictment of the department was in patroling. The commissioner did not know how many men he had on the street at any given time. Men had been assigned for years to a paper district while working in other districts or special squads. Their "commanding officers" had never seen them and their paychecks were forwarded by mail or messenger.

The indictment continued seemingly endlessly. The city had a fine crime lab, but it was staffed largely with men who learned on the job rather than in universities. The communications system was found to be inadequate. During a test period one emergency call waited for 55 rings before being answered. The radio network was so overcrowded with unnecessary calls that a patrolman in a radio car in need of help had to wait up to one minute to contact his headquarters. His chance of making immediate contact was only 50–50.

Poor communications, inadequate training, faulty deployment of the patrol force, impossible community relations were all factors, the report makes clear, in the department's high casualty rate.

Listed here were but a few of the more exaggerated derelictions found by the IACP. When read in its entirety, the survey tended to destroy the department. It criticized the men, their commanders, organization, equipment, training, methods and past achievements. Almost pathetic was this statement concerning the system of commendations: "A casual inspection of forms submitted for awards would indicate . . . a substantial number amounted to nothing more than good, but routine police work." The pathetic became embarrassing when a police captain said during an interview, "I'm probably the most highly commended policeman in the city. I've gotten over 20 commendations and two were the highest the Department gives."

It was discovered that the police depressed the crime rate by ignoring crime reports. If a complainant called in to report a crime, an officer was dispatched to investigate. The choice was his whether to write a report which reached his superiors and was counted in the crime statistics. If he believed the crime was minor or would be difficult to solve, he simply ignored the complaint. Top departmental officers encouraged the practice by constantly exhorting the men to "hold down crime." Much of the crime that went unreported and uninvestigated occurred in the Negro communities of the city, a fact which helped to create resentment against the police.

Other incidents helped the police create, almost without assistance, an explosive racial situation. Acting more like storm troopers than law-enforcement officers, the police carried out nearly 300 midnight raids on Negro homes searching for cop killers whom the FBI found working in a New Jersey zipper factory. The raids were conducted without warrants and on the basis of anonymous tips, creating a situation which Dr. Furman Templeton of the Baltimore Urban League likened to "a state of war."

Negro resentment was intensified by police arrogance toward Negroes, the shortage of Negro policemen and the nearly total absence of high-ranking Negro officers. The situation reached such a low state that the mere appearance of a patrolman in certain Negro districts caused an angry crowd to rise.

Faced with racial problems and revelations of police inefficiency, the city took courageous steps to improve the department. Its first act was to name Lieutenant General George M. Gelston, a commander of the Maryland National Guard, as acting police commissioner. He began to institute reforms, although the department will require years to reshape itself.

General Gelston quickly gave the nation a model for handling racial incidents. He had hardly settled into his seat when the Congress of Racial Equality announced that Baltimore was a national target city. There were large demonstrations aimed at forcing open occupancy in housing and desegregation of taverns.

The scenes that resulted were extremely dangerous. There were giant demonstrations in front of apartment houses and taverns with hundreds of singing, sign-carrying pickets. Straight into this throng marched the Ku Klux Klan in full regalia, with satin hoods and sheets glistening under the street lights. Around was a catcalling crowd of several thousand whites, many of them hoping for a riot.

This happened several times during the spring of 1966 and each time General Gelston took personal command. He kept the three groups separated, often with a cordon of police, endeavoring to protect each group from the other. Traffic was detoured away from the area to aid police control of the situation. General Gelston appeared outwardly calm, seemingly unimpressed by the uproar. Ramrod straight, he strode among his men, patting them on the back, smiling, speaking a few words of encouragement, acting for all the world as if there was nothing to worry about.

General Gelston refused to arrest either civil rightists or Klansmen—and the arrest had been Baltimore's customary "solution" to racial unrest. At one apartment house the demonstration was held under a court injunction limiting pickets to 10 who were orderly and quiet. A hundred noisy pickets showed up and General Gelston immediately lost his ability to count and turned deaf.

Another time demonstrators sat in the street. Newspapers printed the apocryphal story that he detoured traffic around them. Actually the traffic had been detoured first. When the pickets sat in the street, he let them. An inspector asked if the pickets should not be arrested for blocking traffic. General Gelston said he did not see any traffic. After half an hour on the hot asphalt, the demonstrators resumed marching.

Another incident: Demonstrators baited police, trying to get arrested. General Gelston ordered no arrests, which led one demonstrator to say to a reporter, "I'm willing to get arrested. I'm willing to go to jail. But I am not willing to stand out here and march all night."

This was not an exercise in oneupsmanship. General Gelston believes "court injunctions and arrests are an exercise in futility. If you arrest 100 today, there are another 100 tomorrow. Police must remain impartial. People have a constitutional right to demonstrate in this country. The police job is to protect them from harm—and nothing more. My job is to show my men by my own example that they can best control the situation by remaining cool-headed and concentrating on their job, regardless of their personal feelings."

He added: "So far this has worked. It may not always. We may have riots, but I am convinced our course is the only one that will work in the long run."

General Gelston kept the police impartial in racial matters. He kept the demonstration focused on open occupancy and desegregation of public accommodations. The purpose of the demonstration was not sidetracked into police brutality. As a result of this policy, Negro citizens of Baltimore began to look upon policemen as their friends and not their enemies. They asked for no favors, only courtesy and impartiality. With proper leadership at the top, Baltimore began to achieve it.

By so doing, Baltimore made academic one of the biggest controversies in large cities today, that of the civilian review board. Civil-rights leaders have sought to control police brutality by creating a commission of non-policemen to judge the merit of a policeman's actions in arresting a citizen. Almost to a man, police have resisted the board, contending it is unwarranted interference with their affairs and will be detrimental to police morale.

General Gelston's work in Baltimore indicated that, if police handle themselves well, the charge of "police brutality" is seldom heard.

Are other police departments as bad as Baltimore's was? Few, if any, departments have as many problems, but most have some of the problems. For example, one city of over 500,000 population declares its men to be policemen after only one week of training. New York has been plagued periodically with instances in which crimes were not reported. It is certainly no exaggeration of the problem to state that one solution to the mounting crime problem lies in upgrading the standards and efficiency of police departments.

CHAPTER TEN

Water, Air, Health Problems

AMERICA HAS an acute pollution problem. Our air and water, which were pure when settlers came to these shores only three centuries ago and which were only slightly contaminated as recently as 25 years ago, are today poisoned to the point of at least temporary unusability. We have contaminated our environment until we have a shortage of water and, unbelievably, air to breathe. Pollution of water and air will be discussed separately, but they actually are the same problem with similar solutions.

Three quarters of the earth is covered by water. We are blessed with an estimated 1.1 trillion gallons of water. So how can there be a shortage? Most of it is unusable by humans. About 97.2 percent is in the oceans, unfit to drink and too salty even for irrigation. Another 2 percent is frozen in the Arctic and Antarctic ice packs. The remaining fraction of 1 percent is the fresh water in our rivers and streams which supports man and his civilization.

Nearly half of this water used by man goes for irrigation, turning arid fields fertile, deserts into croplands. Another 40 percent is used by industry. It takes 770 gallons of water to refine a barrel of petroleum, 65,000 gallons to produce a ton of steel, 600,000 gallons to manufacture a ton of synthetic rubber. The remaining 10 percent is consumed by humans in drinking, cooking, washing, cleaning and watering lawns.

The problem is not so much that we do not have enough fresh water as that the supplies are unevenly divided. Heavily populated Southern California is chronically short of water—Los Angeles' annual rainfall averages only 11 inches —while Northern California has an abundance. The northern portion has 70 percent of the state's water and allows much of it to run into the sea unused, while Southern California imports billions of gallons a year from the Colorado River at great expense. Recently floods ravaged the Midwest, while the Northeast was experiencing the worst drought in its history.

Because water does not exist where it is needed and because of the weather and man's waste, there is an overall water shortage in the United States. Many areas have perennial rationing, and the situation can only worsen. We presently use 355 billion gallons a day. By the 1980s demand is expected to be 600 billion gallons. By the end of the century we may need 1 trillion gallons.

An overriding consideration in these estimates is that we cannot *make* water. Our planet has all the water it will ever have. We can neither gain nor lose any, for nature moves water in an unchanging cycle. Water evaporates under the heat of the sun, then falls to earth as rain, eventually to rise to the surface again to evaporate anew.

Where, then, will our water supplies come from? We will have to stop wasting what we have, transport water from where it is abundant to where it is needed, and desalinate ocean water.

We waste water as though there were no conceivable end to it. Wasting water is almost an American birthright. But the people of Israel, living in a land where water is precious, have pioneered in its full use and conservation. All water is nationalized in Israel, rationing is enforced, and both its collection and use are controlled by a master plan. The Sea of Galilee and the River Jordan are used together with wells, reservoirs and pipelines. So efficient is the system that 90 percent of all water sources are being used. Since irrigation requires the most water in Israel, hydrologists and agronomists have sought to make best use of available supplies. They have tried to discover just how much water a plant actually needs, to use chemicals to reduce evaporation from the leaves and soil, and to engineer systems to control runoff from fields so it can be used in other areas.

In an industrial society the secret is to reuse the same water several times, just as modern public fountains recirculate the water rather than waste it. The steel industry in West Germany's Ruhr Valley has installed water-circulation systems in its plants to use the same water repeatedly—and has cut water consumption by 98 percent. American firms have hardly begun to even think in these terms.

Less appealing, perhaps, but equally feasible is reuse of water consumed by humans. California, which has one of the best water-conservation programs in the nation, has shown how to halt the dumping of once-used water into the sea. At the Whittier Narrows Water Reclamation Plant, water leaving a conventional sewage system is aerated, filtered and chlorinated until it is not only more savory but almost half again as cheap as water piped from the Colorado River. Because of public sensitivity to drinking reclaimed water, the product of the Whittier Narrows plant is dumped into the ground to raise the natural water table. But clearly, such water could be fed back into the reservoirs. Eventually the U. S. will probably have to do this on a mass scale.

Transporting water from where it is abundant to where it is needed is the principle behind most of our major city water systems. Chicago draws its water from nearby Lake Michigan, but New York taps the Delaware River (ignoring until recently the polluted Hudson River) and reservoirs great distances from the city. Baltimore uses the Susquehanna River, and Los Angeles, the Colorado. Such efforts may have to be greatly increased. New York is considering going all the way to the St. Lawrence River, which forms part of its border with Canada. California is already building the Feather River Project. In 1970 water will be borne from north of Sacramento through pipelines and canals to Los Angeles, providing electric power, flood control and recreational lakes in the process. The system will cost 2.2 billion dollars—a high price—but as water supplies grow shorter, the nation may have no other choice.

Desalination of seawater, long a dream of man, is coming closer to reality. There are about 200 plants in operation around the world using various methods. On the Greek island of Symé, the heat of the sun is used to evaporate the water. In Israel the salt water is frozen, then the water separated from the impurities. Most plants use artificial heat to evaporate the water. Techniques have been improved until engineers can now get one gallon of fresh water from three and a half gallons of seawater. The cost is now about a dollar per gallon, three times the price of natural water. With nuclear power and larger plants, the price of desalinated water should become competitive with natural water. This may occur as the water shortage increases.

But all of these methods will not be enough unless, as a nation, we stop polluting our rivers. We have turned our majestic rivers and lakes into cesspools. Eight children became ill with typhoid fever after eating a watermelon which had floated down the Hudson River to New York. Niagara Falls sometimes smells like rotten eggs. The Potomac River, which was such a joy to George Washington, is posted along its entire length lest someone fall into it and become sickened. The Mississippi, "Father of Waters," has been the scene of repeated "fish kills" where millions of creatures float dead on the water. The Chesapeake Bay oyster crop has dwindled to a tenth of its prepollution size. Gemlike Lake Tahoe, high in the Sierra Nevadas, is threatening to turn from blue to green because of pollution. Lake Erie is so contaminated that parts of it are without oxygen and can support no life. By pollution alone, man has advanced nature's timetable thousands of years in rapidly turning that great lake into a swamp. And these are only a few of the tragedies. It is said that no river, stream, lake or pond in America is without pollution.

We have the technology and wealth to prevent our industrial and sanitary wastes from contaminating our waters. We lack only the will. Where antipollution ordinances have been enforced, spectacular achievements have resulted. The Kimberly-Clark Corporation planned to build a large pulp-and-paper plant in Northern Californaa. The state required that the effluent from the plant be pure enough to prevent harm to newly hatched salmon and trout. The firm installed a 2-million-dollar sewage-disposal system, including a tank in which fish lived in the pure effluent without harm. The Ohio River has shown marked improvement in recent years after antipollution rules were enforced. The Ruhr Valley in West Germany has a cooperative consisting of 250 municipalities and 2,200 industries, the members of which pay the full cost of purifying their effluent.

We have the means to stop pollution. All we need are proper laws and enforcement through well-organized government agencies operating on a regional basis. As it is now, one city builds an adequate treatment plant and enforces antipollution laws, only to have its work undone by communities farther upriver which ignore the problem.

Essentially the same situation applies to air pollution. There are a few technical problems, but in general we know how to stop it. The only problem is to do it.

It seems incredible that there should be a shortage of air. Our planet has enough atmosphere to provide 2.5 million tons of air for each human being. Yet under certain weather conditions, urban dwellers have difficulty breathing the 30 pounds of clean air they need to support life each day. The air is contaminated with carbon monoxide from motor vehicles and other internal combustion engines; sulfur oxides from burning coal and oil in power plants, factories and homes; and hydrocarbons from unburned fuels, particularly in cars. Several of these pollutants are deadly poisons if concentrations are large enough.

In 1963, our atmosphere was estimated to contain 125 million tons of pollutants. Three years later the estimate was 145 million tons. By the end of the century, if the situation goes uncorrected, 250 million tons will be sent aloft. Earth's atmosphere could perhaps handle this load of soot, particles and chemicals if it were evenly distributed. But a weather condition known as an "inversion" periodically traps the fouled air over the area which produces it. An inversion occurs when warm air moves over the top of colder air, thus disrupting the normal cycle in which warm air rises to the top. The air remains stationary for days and a thick haze of pollutants settles over the area. In 1952, an inversion lasting only four days killed 4,000 people in London. In 1948, a similar inversion sickened 43 percent of the people of Donora, Pennsylvania, a small mining and industrial town near Pittsburgh. Twenty people died. New York City lost 400 residents in an inversion in 1963.

Even without inversions the simple day-to-day breathing of foul air causes serious health problems. "There is no doubt," said John Gardner, the U. S. Secretary of Health, Education, and Welfare, "that air pollution is a contributing factor in the rising incidence of chronic respiratory diseases— lung cancer, emphysema, bronchitis and asthma."

Los Angeles has shown the rest of the country how to cope with air pollution, perhaps because its problems were worse than elsewhere. The Los Angeles area forms a natural basin. Mountains surround it on three sides, and onshore breezes from the ocean tend to trap the air over the area. With Los Angeles' great growth in industry and population, the still air rapidly became contaminated. "Smog" in "sunny California" became a national joke—and a distinct health hazard to the people living there.

Improvement began when Los Angeles residents demanded it. A stiff antipollution law was enacted and an expert staff recruited to enforce it. Open burning and crude incineration of refuse were forbidden. Oil refineries, power plants and factories were required to install smoke-control and antipollution devices which met rigid standards. When forced to, the industrial firms outdid themselves in redesigning their manufacturing techniques and in inventing pollution-control equipment. Some firms found that the smoke which had been thrown off into the atmosphere contained chemicals which could be recovered and sold at a profit, thus paying for the cost of the equipment.

Los Angeles discovered, however, that the automobile is the biggest contaminator of the air. Each car produces 7 pounds of wastes a day. Beginning with the 1966 models, all new cars sold in California are required to have antipollution devices. The federal government subsequently enacted a law requiring such equipment on all 1968 model cars sold in this country. The vehicular devices are not perfect, but engineers expect to improve them.

Even if all that could be done to control air pollution is done, the day may come when use of the gas-burning engine will need to be restricted in urban areas in favor of the electric car. Automobile manufacturers, chemical and petroleum companies and other firms are investing huge sums to perfect such a car. The technical problem is to lengthen the life and range of the battery. Researchers are confident that by the mid-1970s they will have perfected batteries which will permit a vehicle to cruise for extended periods at 50 miles an hour. Most urban planners look upon the electric car as a salvation, for it will eliminate not only odors and pollution, but noise as well.

If neglect and abuse of our water and air have led to our present serious problems, there is room for optimism. National publicity campaigns have aroused public awareness of the dangers. All levels of government have taken steps to cope with pollution. A great deal more needs to be done by government and especially by industry and private individuals, but we are beginning to preserve our irreplaceable natural resources, lending hope to the future.

Our pollution problems are part of a series of larger difficulties which might be categorized under "health." Our chief urban health problems are those illnesses and infirmities which plague mankind: heart disease, cancer, old age, mental retardation, tuberculosis and several others. These are medical problems and not the province of this book, except insofar as poverty, malnutrition, poor housing and inferior sanitation cause them. Since the need to end poverty and eliminate ghettos has already been discussed, we can go on to another health problem which might better be termed the "hospital problem."

The headline cited in the opening chapter ("OUR HOSPITALS ARE KILLING US") indicates the public attention which has focused on our hospitals. The headline is highly inaccurate and grossly unfair, but the fact remains that our medical institutions are in trouble.

Chief among the problems is obsolescence. Many of our hospitals are old, built in horse-and-buggy days when hospitals were thought of as hotels to recuperate (or die) in and modern technological and scientific medicine was undreamed of. Unfortunately, some of the newer hospitals were built under this old concept.

These hospitals are grossly inefficient. When a patient comes into a hospital seriously ill or for major surgery, he needs a few days of intensive care. Then, as he recuperates, he needs progressively less care. Many hospitals have set up intensive-care wards and postoperative recovery rooms are routine, but basically our hospitals were built improperly. Patients are bedded in rooms and wards off long corridors, frequently long distances from nurses and doctors who are on duty. Intensive care becomes most difficult. Little discrimination is possible between the severely ill and the recuperating. Postoperative patients receive—and pay for—a great deal of food and other hotel-type services they cannot use, while recuperating patients have close nursing attendance they don't need.

Monitoring equipment is available today to register pulse and heartbeat, temperature, respiration and other data automatically, thus permitting a single attendant to keep close watch on the minute-by-minute condition of several seriously ill patients. But installing such equipment in older hospitals, if possible at all, would be prohibitively expensive.

Our vintage medical buildings were not constructed with modern sanitary problems in mind. Hospitals face a severe threat from bacteria resistant to modern antibiotics, such as penicillin. So great is the danger that one out of every 8 surgical patients becomes infected. Some of this is carelessness on the part of hospital personnel. Lulled into a false sense of security by the belief that modern drugs had ended the bacterial threat, surgeons and nurses sometimes are careless about scrubbing. They use rubber gloves that are split, fail to change face masks, touch unsanitary equipment. Unauthorized persons enter the operating room. But at the same time, vintage buildings provide safe harbors for germs in cracks in the walls, floors, ceramic tile, light fixtures, and furniture where they escape the most determined disinfecting team. Modern hospitals could reduce the number of such hiding places.

Our obsolete buildings should be replaced with modern, properly designed structures. In these the intensive-care patients would be gathered in circular wards, where they could be under constant surveillance by nursing personnel. Monitoring equipment would be affixed. In a few days patients would be moved to recuperative wings where less intensive care could be provided. Operating rooms could be built with sanitary considerations in mind and linked with the necessary radiological, laboratory and other equipment. The plain truth today is that some lives are lost because the blood supplies, drugs and equipment are scattered all over the hospital and not available when an emergency develops.

We need new, better designed hospitals not only to provide better care and make use of modern medical science, but also to handle more patients. Overcrowding of urban hospitals ranges from the severe to the disreputable. Waiting lists for admission and beds in hallways are common. With Medicare, under which elderly citizens can receive the care they need, and with our growing population, the situation is worsening.

Another difficult problem is the chronic shortage of nurses and other hospital personnel. Nurses are overworked, underpaid, harassed by nonnursing tasks that are pure drudgery and unappreciated. Several abuses result. Overtaxed nurses make mistakes, administering the wrong medication, failing to operate equipment in accordance with instructions, neglecting patients who desperately need attention. Improperly trained personnel, such as student nurses and aides, take over whole wards on some shifts, while in another wing nurses are emptying bedpans and serving food, duties properly performed by less highly trained personnel.

Correcting the shortage of nurses will not be easy. Finding the money to pay them what they are worth and shortening their work load so as to attract more men and women into the profession are the most likely solution. There is evidence that nursing training leaves a lot to be desired. The three years of training could be concentrated perhaps into one year, with more classroom work and study and less ward duty. More specialization among nurses seems warranted, so that those caring for recuperative patients could receive less training than surgical or intensive-care nurses. They could specialize as physicians do in surgery, internal medicine, pediatrics, obstetrics. Such specialization, if it did not permit shorter training, might turn out better nurses. Then there seems to be a far greater need for practical nurses, aides, orderlies, secretaries and clerks to unburden the medically trained so they can perform the jobs they are best qualified to do.

The high cost of hospital care is a problem affecting every American family. In 1966, President Johnson called for a federal investigation of rising medical costs after receiving a report that hospital and doctor bills had risen 3.4 percent in a year. A study in the New York area made this a minimal figure. The charges for a 10-day stay in a semiprivate room in that city increased from 560 dollars to 842 dollars. Within a year it was expected to be almost 1,000 dollars.

There are several reasons for the rising medical costs. Personnel is a major one. With obsolete buildings that preclude automation, hospitals must hire three to four employees for every patient. The employees rightly demand higher wages, which tax hospital finances. The new life-saving equipment used in surgery and laboratories is expensive. The apparatus for open-heart surgery costs more than 100,000 dollars. The price hospitals pay for drugs and medications is higher. Indeed, the cost of everything a hospital uses has gone up.

Another major reason for the rising costs is the widespread practice of overcharging those patients able to pay to compensate for those who cannot or do not pay. Thus in New York, if a paying patient spends 10 days in a voluntary hospital (as distinct from a publicly-owned hospital), he pays 842 dollars. If the patient is on welfare, the hospital receives only 504 dollars from the city government. The higher bill for the paying patients reflects the loss taken on the welfare patient. In 1964, New York hospitals lost 17 million dollars treating indigent patients in clinics and wards. What exists, then, is a system wherein the rich patient pays for the poor (a form of taxation) and the healthy subscriber to an insurance plan such as Blue Cross helps support the more sickly subscriber.

It is argued that this system is unfair, that our hospitals waste money in inefficient administration, by purchasing equipment they don't use, by performing unnecessary surgery and by harboring patients who are not sick enough to warrant hospital treatment. Abuses doubtlessly exist, but even if they were all corrected, it is still obvious that our hospitals need financial help. They need money both for buildings and for expenses. Barring a huge increase in philanthropy, the funds can come only from rising hospital bills or from larger governmental appropriations.

CHAPTER ELEVEN

Traffic and Transit

WHEN THE SOCIAL HISTORY of our times is written centuries from now, the American and his automobile will be one of its absurdities. We pay 2,000 to 5,000 dollars for a giant car with a 300-"horse" engine capable of cruising at 120 miles an hour. We license it, insure it, fill it with several dollars' worth of gasoline, get on a 100-million-dollar urban expressway—often paying a toll—squeeze into a lane of traffic and zoom off at all of 5 miles an hour. We ultimately arrive home an hour late, nerves exhausted, emotions drained, to settle down to a cold dinner. That tens of millions of Americans endure the situation every working day is one of the mysteries of our times.

Perhaps we endure highway congestion because we assume that nothing can be done about it. The truth is a great deal can be done. Perhaps we endure it because we feel there is no suitable alternative. There may not be an alternative, but there could be.

The urban traffic problem needs little description. No one living in or near a city can help but know about it. But some figures may give additional magnitude to it. In 1962 there were 78 million registered motor vehicles and Americans drove 713 billion passenger miles, computed by multiplying passengers by miles of travel. In 1964 there were 86 million motor vehicles. If the trend continues, there will be 120 million vehicles in 1980.

The crush of cars is more than an inconvenience. There are nearly 50,000 highway fatalities each year. The noxious fumes and noise destroy much of the livability of our cities. Congestion dampens commercial activity and wastes stupendous sums of money by delaying the movement of men and materials.

One other characteristic of our traffic problem should be cited. The car has an impact in rural as well as urban areas, but the problem is worse in urban areas because 50 percent of the vehicles use 10 percent of the urban streets and highways.

What can we do about the traffic problem?

One pie-in-the-sky solution often suggested is to get rid of the cars in cities and return the streets to pedestrians. People so minded have suggested that city traffic be restricted by high taxes, special tolls and even embargoes. Stop the cars at the outskirts and don't allow them in.

Henry A. Barnes, Traffic Commissioner for the City of New York and perhaps the nation's most pragmatic traffic expert, denounces such schemes as both impractical and foolhardy. The motor vehicle, he says, is vital to the economic life of our cities. Nearly all food supplies and other goods are borne in and out of the city by truck. Most of the services on which urban dwellers depend are supplied by motor vehicle. Removing cars from cities will also remove most of the tourists, shoppers, patrons at cultural, recreational and athletic events, salesmen, doctors and other professional men, and many others too numerous to name here.

Assuredly, the nonessential traffic should be removed. The fellow who lives in the suburbs and drives his car to work, parks it in a garage and drives home ought to have an alternative means of transportation. But the traffic essential to the commercial life of the city still poses a problem of great magnitude.

The automobile is a fixture in American life and seems certain to remain so. Eighty percent of all American families own at least one car. In urban areas, the percentage of car-owning families ranges from a low of 72 percent in Chicago to a high of 91 percent in San Jose, California, and in the latter city 37 percent own more than one car. Owning a car is an American birthright—and a necessity. Sixty-four percent of the population use the car to get to and from work. The car is a symbol of affluence, a source of pleasure, and an island of privacy in a crowded world. It supports several giant industries, such as automobile manufacturers and makers of rubber and petroleum. The car *is* now and *will be* in the future.

But so is the urban-transportation problem. Our principal solution to the problem has been to build highways. In the decade ending in 1965, approximately 43.6 billion dollars was spent on urban highways. In the next 20 years, another 52.5 billion dollars will be needed, for a total of nearly 100 billion dollars. Nationwide, about 297 billion dollars is expected to be spent on highways.

The cost of urban highways is staggering. Just 3 miles of the Central Artery in Boston cost 125 million dollars. Chicago invested 50 million dollars in 8 miles of the Congress Street Expressway. Ten miles of the Hollywood Freeway in Los Angeles cost 55 million dollars. In Detroit the first 24 miles of the expressway system required an expenditure of over 200 million dollars. The Cross-Bronx Expressway in New York City cost 22,450 dollars a mile.

Despite all of the effort and expense, several serious mistakes have been made. First, we built four- to eight-lane superhighways linking the central cities with the outskirts without making adequate provision for the cars when they left the expressway. The cars reach the exit ramp and then creep over narrow, congested, neglected city streets.

Second, we tried, certainly in the early highway-building days, to make highways serve a dual purpose: to move traffic and to serve stores and industry along the way. Highway engineers now agree that the two purposes cannot mesh. Multilane highways with unlimited access to roadside stores and factories have turned into death traps. The fatality rate on the Boston Post Road in Connecticut is three times that on the Merritt Parkway, the earliest limited-access highway. Seven times as many people are killed on U. S. Route 1 in Maine as on the Maine Turnpike. Not only are open-access roads a safety hazard, they are inefficient. Studies show that cars move almost twice as fast on an urban highway with controlled access as on uncontrolled roads.

Our third mistake was in assuming that new highways would solve the urban-transportation problem. Cities have discovered that, as soon as a new or improved highway is opened, it becomes congested almost immediately. Motorists flock to take advantage of the new route and a traffic problem soon emerges.

We cannot possibly build highways fast enough to accommodate the increasing number of vehicles. Not only is the cost great, but the roads shrink the tax base and remove land badly needed for housing and other facilities. One possible solution, advocated by Mr. Barnes, is to double-deck certain expressways to make greater use of the same land. But whatever is done, it is plain that our urban transportation problem cannot be solved by building expressways. A modern highway system is essential to the city, but we must at the same time improve the traffic flow and develop mass-transit facilities.

The movement of vehicles over our city streets, as distinct from expressways—in a word, *traffic*—is a national disgrace. As with other problems, we have the means and the know-how to move vehicles far more efficiently than we do now, but we simply do not do it. It is amazing that long-suffering motorists have not insisted on better traffic control. Instead, with few exceptions, only a minuscule fraction of the municipal budget goes for traffic control. Until recently, Bridgeport, Connecticut, city of 100,000, spent only 17,000 dollars a year on traffic control. Detroit still regulates its traffic lights with a Tokheim Controller—last built in 1928. Traffic engineers are hamstrung, not only by lack of funds, but by rigid political controls. In Chicago, for example, every traffic regulation, except those for speed, must be approved by a separate ordinance of the City Council—and speed regulations are voted on by the state legislature. If the Chicago traffic director wishes to install a stop sign or a traffic light, or make a street one-way he must get a bill through the Council. The first essential to improved traffic is an adequate traffic department, properly staffed, empowered to act and sufficiently solvent to do the job.

The most obvious action which must take place to improve traffic is to begin using 100 percent of the street space. At present we use between 25 and 50 percent of our streets for traffic. The rest is used for parking, loading zones, cab stands, bus stops, parades, jaywalkers and vendors. We have a talent for converting a 6-lane thoroughfare into a traffic problem. Curbside parking reduces it to two lanes, then double-parking and motorists trying to park lower it to one lane in either direction, one third of capacity.

One way to reduce the problem may be to prohibit curb parking. The concept that a city should provide garage facilities on the public streets will probably be changed sooner or later. Most cities endeavor to enforce no-parking regulations on downtown streets during rush hours, but this practice should be extended to many peripheral and residential areas. Congestion on these streets adds to traffic jams on thoroughfares. Many of the side streets could be used as auxiliary routes through the city if parking was prohibited.

The idea of free public parking on city residential streets —or metered parking—is so ingrained that no municipal government has had the political courage to ban the practice. Eventually, the sheer crush of cars may force the decision. Where will private cars be parked? In off-street garages. It seems unlikely that cities will be able to provide such facilities at public expense. It is most likely that city motorists will have to accept the necessity of paying considerably more than they do now to park their cars. Private capital (or cooperatives) may have to erect parking facilities in apartment- or row-house areas. Motorists may have to pay a rather high price to garage their cars. There seems to be no other alternative.

The next biggest waste of street space is the truck-loading zone. In most of our cities, the curb space on the most congested streets is taken over by trucks delivering and picking up merchandise at stores and apartment houses. Cities, if they had the courage, could improve the traffic flow a great deal right now by simply restricting deliveries to the hours between 6 P.M. and 8 A.M. Evening, night and early-morning deliveries would pose an inconvenience for merchants, but improve traffic noticeably. A more permanent improvement would be to clear out the middle of certain blocks and install truck-terminal facilities. The storekeepers fronting on four sides of the block would accept deliveries through the rear.

That these relatively simple procedures have not been carried out is a measure of the neglect of the traffic problem. As a nation, we act as though we would rather lament the traffic than do anything about it.

We could greatly improve our traffic situation if we made use of the technological equipment that is available. I was living in Baltimore when Henry Barnes installed an electronic traffic-signal system, one of the first in the nation. The 4.5-million-dollar system replaced a 69-dollar master controller which hung on the wall of the men's room in Police Headquarters. The new system increased traffic volume by 300 percent and cut travel time by one third.

Unless electronic traffic control has been experienced, the motorist cannot grasp just how bad the older systems are. Have you ever driven down a busy street and stopped for a red light on a cross street and waited—only to have not a single car use the green light on the side street? Have you ever driven in a town where there are signs reading, "Lights timed for 25 mph" and laughed because the street was so crowded you could not go over 15 mph unless you had wings? These are but two of the scores of abuses under older traffic-signal systems. The lights change on a regular basis, whether the traffic warrants it or not. One antique system uses a punched tape to control the lights. The tape is programmed so that on Tuesday at 5 P.M., for example, the traffic signals will change to give more green to the busy streets and less to the cross streets. This may work on some

Tuesdays, but not if traffic lets out early or there is an accident or a fire tying up traffic or if a ballgame ends and thrusts a burst of cars into the area. The lights are fixed. No changes can be made.

With the electronic systems, the controller actually counts the cars using the streets, adjusts the cycle of lights to give the green where it is needed most—and does it automatically within seconds. Lights can be timed to fit the speed of traffic, because, when traffic is heavy, it moves slower. Thus, instead of 25 mph, the lights can be adjusted to 10 or 15 mph. The signal system can be automatically adjusted to favor inbound traffic in the morning and outbound at night, to speed the movement of cars on heavily traveled two-way streets. A sudden surge of traffic from a parking lot or stadium benefits from rapid adjustment of lights to clear out the area. If streets are icy, the lights fit the traffic pattern. These modern systems can make hundreds of automatic adjustments to the needs of the moment.

When I lived in Baltimore, I discovered that, under the electronic system (dubbed the "Barnes Brain"), I could drive from the center of the city seven miles to the suburbs without stopping for a red light—until I reached the suburbs, which didn't have the new system. As a general rule, if a person drove straight ahead on a street with the flow of traffic, only an occasional red light was encountered. As soon as the motorist made a turn, he encountered a red light. Then, if he continued in that direction, he had only green lights. Traffic, while heavy, flowed smoothly.

Mr. Barnes is installing a similar, 100-million-dollar system in New York. A number of other cities have electronic systems. Their application will eventually become universal.

The New York Traffic Commissioner insists that we have the technological capability to increase the efficiency and safety of urban expressways by applying electronics to the family car. The vehicle needs power brakes, power steering, carburetor controls and a "little black box." If a coaxial cable were installed along the road, it would control the movement of the cars. The cable would be programmed so that cars moved at a prearranged speed and stayed a set distance apart, depending upon weather and traffic conditions. The little black box, taking its electronic instructions from the cable, would control the car's speed, its distance from the car in front and its ability to turn out of lane. If a driver tried to go too fast, the accelerator would be inactivated and the brakes automatically applied. If he tried to turn out of lane in a no-passing zone, the power steering would become inoperative. As long as he stayed with the flow of traffic and in lane, he would drive normally. The electronic system would become operative only to prevent him from making mistakes. Mr. Barnes believes that, as traffic volumes increase, such a system will become mandatory.

But even if our cities make all the improvements in traffic control and movement that they possibly can, our street space will be inadequate to the demands of the future. The principal solution to our urban transportation problem lies in large increases in mass-transit facilities. In fact, it may be stated that the growth of the transportation problem has kept pace with the decline in mass-transit facilities.

Leaving out the artificial years of World War II, we find that, in 1940, mass transit carried about 95 million passengers—a number equal to the U. S. urban population at that time. In 1950, there were about 112 million passengers. Today there are a little over 60 million passengers. Between 1954 and 1963, 194 transit companies went out of business. Sizeable towns are without any facilities. Net revenue from transit operations in the U. S. has shrunk to 75 million dollars, less than half the 1950 figure. Where transit operations made an average 4.6 percent profit on their revenue in 1950, they are losing money today. There are a few exceptional cities where transit operations are thriving, but the national trend is bleak.

To begin to understand the reasons for the plight of transit in this country, as well as the need for improved facilities, examine the following table. It shows the percentage of residents who use public transportation to get to and from their work in cities. Central-city and suburban residents are separated.

City	Percent from Central City	Percent from Suburbs
New York	65	23
Los Angeles	13	4
Chicago	43	16
Philadelphia	44	13
Detroit	22	5
San Francisco	33	8
Boston	43	18
Pittsburgh	34	15
Washington, D. C.	42	12
Cleveland	32	14
Baltimore	30	7
Newark	42	20
Minneapolis	21	5
Seattle	19	3
San Diego	8	2
Denver	15	3
Phoenix	5	3
Fort Worth	10	1
Over 1,000,000 Population (metropolitan area)	30	12
500,000 to 1,000,000	18	6
300,000 to 500,000	15	4
250,000 to 300,000	13	4
200,000 to 250,000	11	3
Under 100,000	6	3

This table shows that among our major cities only minorities of suburbanites use public transportation to and from work and that, except for New York, no city has half its central-city residents using public facilities to their jobs. The table also shows that the nonuse of mass transit is markedly greater in smaller than in larger cities.

Why have workers deserted public transportation for the private automobile? The pleasures and privacy and greater mobility of the car are factors certainly. Even if traffic is congested, the motorist has the car to himself. He can listen to the radio and stop at will to run errands or shop. The discomfort of public transportation also drives workers away. Whether by wheel or rail, the facilities are overcrowded, dirty, noisy and slow. An hour on a crowded bus somehow seems longer than an hour behind the wheel.

There is ample evidence that, when transit operations install new equipment and institute faster and more frequent service, they attract back the automobile drivers. But under present conditions, transit operations, whether privately or publicly owned, have a difficult time improving service.

A major problem is peak-hour demand. The commuter railroads of Philadelphia carry 44 percent of their daily traffic in just one hour, 5 to 6 P.M. Rapid transit carries a quarter of its volume in the same hour. The morning and evening rush hours require transit operators to have a great deal of equipment on hand which is used only a part of the day. The Metropolitan Transit Authority in Boston reported that only one third of its buses were used all day—and carried 53 percent of all the passengers. Another one third went into service with the approach of rush hours and out of service when they were over and carried one third of the passengers. The remaining one third of the buses operated only during four peak hours and accounted for 14 percent of the passenger volume. Transit operations, moreover, must cope with peak days. Ours is a five-day work week. On weekends transit operations all but stop.

The traffic problem which plagues the motorist also hounds the bus company. Buses must inch through the same traffic jams, causing them to render slow and expensive service. The Seattle transit operation discovered that a one-mile-an-hour increase in bus speed lowered operating costs 10 percent. Transit firms are also forced to maintain unprofitable routes into the suburbs, and municipal governments have until recently considered them fair game for taxation. A survey of 100 large transit companies showed they pay an average of 9 percent of their revenues in taxes, with the highest being 22 percent. Then, transit companies have to meet higher costs for wages and salaries, fuel, equipment and supplies.

As a result of their financial squeeze, transit operations have been forced to operate obsolete equipment, pay low wages, trim service and raise fares. The average fare is now almost three times what it was in 1947. Several cities now charge 30 and 35 cents for a fare. And high fares mean less patronage. It would seem that whatever transit operators do these days is wrong.

The very low state of public transit in the United States almost qualifies as a national emergency. The need to move people rather than vehicles is great, and our ability to do this is woefully limited despite considerable effort to help transit firms. One step taken by municipalities has been to try to ease the path of transit buses through traffic. Special bus lanes have worked successfully. Enforcement of bus-stop parking regulations, midblock rather than end-of-block bus stops, staggered office hours (notably in Washington, D. C.) have all assisted. Cities have tried to subsidize transit companies by reducing franchise, gross receipts and fuel taxes, by purchasing and leasing equipment to the companies and by other arrangements. While these steps help, the efforts are too little and too late.

More encouraging has been the trend toward public ownership of transit facilities. Private, taxpaying companies have a difficult time. Public ownership, either by the city itself or by an authority, offers definite advantages. Overlapping service between competing companies is eliminated. Notable savings result because the public operation does not have to pay income, sales and fuel taxes, purchase licenses and other fees. This saving can be used for new equipment and improved service. If the public operation is efficiently run, the riders benefit from a changed attitude. Gone is the profit incentive, replaced by a service goal. The public views the transit company not as an unfriendly private firm, but as its own.

A companion trend to public ownership has been local regulation of transit. Traditionally, transit companies were regulated by the state public-utility agency, which is often rurally dominated and less sensitive to urban needs. Several states have relinquished regulation to municipalities, permitting more sensitive control.

Any long-range solution to the mass-transit crisis should take into consideration several steps. One, certainly, is metropolitan-area control. A transit company operates throughout the cities and towns of a metropolitan area. All citizens use the service and therefore unified control of routes, schedules and fares would be desirable. It makes no sense to install a bus lane in one town, if another does not. By pooling financial resources the adjacent municipalities can raise the capital necessary for improved transit.

An example of a regional approach to mass transit is occurring in San Francisco. In 1951, the California legislature established the San Francisco Bay Area Rapid Transit Commission and empowered it to recommend a master transit plan. Studies showed that mass transit was essential. By 1970, San Francisco would need 48 lanes of expressways to handle anticipated peak-hour traffic at principal points. Ten to 12 lanes would be needed to accommodate vehicles crossing the Bay.

The Commission decided to invest in a 1-billion-dollar subway system, to be completed by 1971. It will consist of 75 miles of double track, including 31 miles of elevated structures, 14 miles of surface routes and 16 miles of tunnels. Voters in San Francisco, Alameda and Contra Costa counties authorized a 792-million-dollar bond issue in 1962 to start the project. The rest of the financing will be through revenue bonds.

San Francisco's system will be modern. Seventy-mile-an-hour electric trains will run automatically, their central controls connected to a computer. Greater safety, efficiency and economy are expected to result. Regular users will carry individually coded credit cards which they will insert in a slot to enter the turnstiles. Passengers will be billed monthly. This system, plus automatic change-making devices, will eliminate the need for ticket sellers and other station personnel.

San Francisco's efforts have been the most ambitious, but other metropolitan areas have and are moving toward regional solutions of transit problems.

What type of mass transit? Bus, train, subway, trolley? This is a major concern to transportation planners. The high cost of subways make them rather unfeasible. San Francisco is spending 13 million dollars a mile for its system, with the tunnels costing vastly more than that. An increase in rail transportation is essential, nevertheless. Many more commuter trains (and better ones) on railroads are needed. High-speed trolley service (such as Cleveland's Rapid Transit System operates) has a role. Rail lines need to be extended to other populated areas and improved to permit higher speeds. Rail service needs to be integrated with bus service, so that riders can hop on a bus which deposits them at a convenient suburban rail depot. Another improvement would be convenient parking at such depots so suburbanites could leave their cars at the station, rather than driving downtown to work.

What about the monorail? Perhaps someday, but in the foreseeable future the monorail remains impractical. It is basically the old elevated train in new clothing, and cities eliminated the "el" years ago. The monorail needs an above-ground structure. There must be stations and platforms reaching up to the track. The effect would be rather unsightly. But performance is the biggest obstacle. The monorail at the New York World's Fair went 8 miles an hour and cost 90 cents for a 4,000-foot ride. Disneyland's monorail sways so much it is difficult to remain seated at speeds over 20 miles an hour. The monorail at the Seattle exposition has had serious maintenance problems. The best in operation so far is in Germany, but it carries only 9 million passengers a year. In comparison, the New York subway system carries 6 million a day. To be practical, the monorail needs a switching system, a method by which express and local trains can run on the same track, and some means to lower a disabled car so the rails are not blocked.

Most rapid transit for decades to come will be by bus, a flexible means of travel because the bus can use any street at any time. But there must be sharp improvement in bus service. New equipment, faster and more frequent service, less crowding are all necessary. There must be more express service between suburban points and downtown or factory areas. Such express service needs to be linked with suburban parking facilities, so a suburbanite can drive to a predesignated location, park and hop on a bus that whisks him downtown with a minimum of stops and delay.

To improve bus service a radical change in the bus itself may be necessary. Henry Barnes has called the present bus "the most inefficient piece of mechanical gear ever fashioned by man." It weighs 16 to 18 tons and has a large diesel engine in back and a torque converter. The driver leaves the curb, and the engine just about reaches the point of efficiency when the bus stops again. The vehicle gets only 1½ to 2 miles to a gallon of fuel and fills the streets with black smoke and pollutants. Wear on brakes and the engine is immense. Besides, the bus can only load and unload passengers from one side—meaning that buses can use only one curb on a one-way street. Passengers have to climb two steps to reach the seats. Drivers act like the proverbial one-armed paperhanger, steering, making change and issuing transfer slips.

Mr. Barnes insists there is absolutely no reason that proper transit buses are not built. He would put the motor in a soundproof compartment at the rear and run it at a constant speed which is most efficient. The motor would operate the generator which fuels electric drive in each of the four wheels. This is precisely the principle of the diesel locomotive. The resultant bus would have better traction and faster acceleration. Using the motor for dynamic braking would reduce wear on the brakes and other systems. Such a bus would be quiet, efficient and economical. Since it would have a lower center of gravity, it would be easier to enter and leave. Those steps could be eliminated. If the driver were installed in the center, doors could be placed on either side.

Mr. Barnes has suggested to bus manufacturers that they design such vehicles, but has gotten the reply that no one has ever ordered it. This is only one example of the nonsensical in urban transportation. Another is the fact that the more than 2 million residents of Brooklyn, New York, have no intercity bus station. If they wish to take a Greyhound or Trailways bus, they, along with the residents of the Bronx, Queens and Staten Island, must journey to the most congested spot on earth, mid-Manhattan.

These examples, supplied by Mr. Barnes during interviews, are indicative of the absence of planning in mass transportation. There may be no ultimate solution until an integrated plan, involving highways, parking, railroads, trolleys, and buses, is developed for a metropolitan area. Operation as well as planning should be integrated. Finances should be pooled so that highway revenues aid transit and vice versa.

Expenditures for mass transit must be greatly enlarged. We have spent hundreds of billions of dollars for highways but only paltry sums for transit. The balance must be corrected or transportation in this country will continue its slide into chaos.

CHAPTER TWELVE

A Last Look at Perspective

IN THIS BOOK an attempt has been made to cover the major urban problems. There are others which might be added. Our cities need improved recreational facilities. Beautification is a prime need, along with cultural facilities, universities, centers for science and the arts. More briefly stated, we need to make our cities more livable and more beautiful. We even need to build new cities that eliminate the problems of the older ones. Some urban planners have said that hundreds of model cities, such as Reston in Virginia and Columbia in Maryland, must be built in decades to come. These are not housing developments, but complete cities with people of various income levels, factories, stores, a downtown and suburbs, schools, colleges and hospitals.

This book, like nearly all books on urban problems, has discussed the problems separately. We have a housing problem, a poverty problem, a transportation problem, and so on. Each is different and challenging to solve.

But if we look at the problems as a totality, we can see that the common denominator of all our urban problems is neglect. We have neglected housing, poverty, pollution, transportation and the rest. We have neglected to plan, to be efficient, to consider better ways, to spend the necessary funds. Our urban problems are an accumulation of decades of neglect.

The various problems also have common solutions. We need metropolitan-area government and planning. We need imagination, a willingness to innovate. Every single problem will be solved when aroused public opinion demands a solution and the enlightened and powerful men of the community unite to dedicate themselves to a solution. All the solutions involve money, great sums of money from federal, state, local and private sources. Continued niggardliness means no solutions are possible. Thus, the beginnings of our attack on urban problems are the finding of money, the arousing of public opinion, and the organization of leadership for action.

As we have seen, a substantial number of cities have already organized their leadership for community action and found ways to enlist public support. The success in those cities has provided guidelines for other cities to use. Too, we have seen that many individuals, industries and government officials are beginning to innovate in a search for solutions. At this writing, the necessary money is still not available. But government at all levels has recently become aware of the amount of money needed and how it might best be used. The search for new sources of revenue and better use of available funds continues.

At long last the historic pattern of neglect of our cities and their problems has been broken. From the White House to city hall, from the urban planner to the man on the street, there is a new awareness of the problems of our cities and the promise that will be fulfilled by their solution.

We have discussed many separate urban problems, the solution of which will be difficult. The sum of the individual problems can easily be disheartening. But if, with perspective, we look at our problems as a totality, we can see in the ending of neglect, the marshaling of leadership, the search for ideas and financing grounds for encouragement and optimism.

Suggested Reading

THE FOLLOWING TITLES were selected from a large body of literature, in part because they express viewpoints in disagreement with some of those in this book.

ABRAMS, CHARLES. *The City Is the Frontier.* New York: Harper & Row, 1965.

ANDERSON, MARTIN. *The Federal Bulldozer.* Cambridge, Mass.: Massachusetts Institute of Technology Press, 1964.

BARNES, HENRY A. *The Man with the Red and Green Eyes.* New York: E. P. Dutton Co., 1965.

BRIDENBAUGH, CARL. *Cities in Revolt.* New York: Alfred Knopf Inc., 1955.

ECKBO, GARRETT. *Urban Landscape Design.* New York: McGraw-Hill Inc., 1964.

FETTERMAN, ROBERT A. *The Fate of Our Cities.* Garden City, N. Y.: Doubleday, 1961.

GOODMAN, CHARLES M. *Life for Dead Spaces.* New York: Harcourt, Brace & World, 1963.

GORDON, MITCHELL. *Sick Cities.* New York: Macmillan Co., 1963.

GOTTMAN, JEAN. *Megalopolis.* New York: Twentieth Century Fund, 1961.

GREEN, CONSTANCE. *The Rise of Urban America.* New York: Harper & Row, 1965.

GREER, SCOTT A. *Urban Renewal and the American City.* Indianapolis, Ind.: Bobbs-Merrill, 1966.

GRUEN, VICTOR. *The Heart of Our Cities.* New York: Simon & Schuster, 1964.

HIGBEE, EDWARD C. *The Squeeze.* New York: William Morrow & Co., 1960.

JACOBS, JANE. *The Death and Life of Great American Cities.* New York: Random House, 1961.

MEYERSON, MARTIN. *Face of the Metropolis.* New York: Random House, 1963.

MUMFORD, LEWIS. *The Culture of Cities.* New York: Harcourt, Brace & Co., 1963.

OWEN, WILFRED. *The Metropolitan Transportation Problem.* Washington, D. C.: The Brookings Institution, 1956.

RAYMORE, HENRY B., and ORTLOFF, H. STUART. *It's Your Community.* New York: M. Barrows, 1965.

SMERK, GEORGE M. *Urban Transportation; The Federal Role.* Bloomington, Ind.: Indiana University Press, 1965.

WEAVER, ROBERT C. *Dilemmas of Urban America.* Cambridge, Mass.: Harvard University Press, 1965.

———. *The Urban Complex.* Garden City, N. Y.: Doubleday & Co., 1964.

Index

THIS BOOK WAS SET IN

CALEDONIA AND TORINO TYPE,

PRINTED AND BOUND BY

H. WOLFF BOOK MANUFACTURING CO., INC.

IT WAS DESIGNED BY

BARBARA LIMAN.